KU-616-948

COUNTDOWN
BUMPER
PUZZLE BOOK

COUNTDOWN
BUMPER
PUZZLE BOOK

GRANADA

Countdown is the creation of Armond Jammot;
It is a Yorkshire Television production

First published in Great Britain in 2002
By Granada Media, an imprint of Andre Deutsch Ltd
20 Mortimer Street
London W1T 3JW

In association with Granada Media Group

Text and photographs copyright © Granada Media Group Ltd, 2002

The right of Michael Wylie and Damian Eadie to be identified as the
authors of this work has been asserted by them in accordance with the
Copyright, Designs and Patents Act 1988.

All rights reserved. This book is sold subject to the condition that it
may not be reproduced, stored in a retrieval system or transmitted in
any form or by any means, electronic, mechanical photocopying,
recording or otherwise without the publisher's prior consent.

A catalogue record of this book is available from the British Library

ISBN 0 233 05104 X

3 5 7 9 10 8 6 4 2

Typeset by E-Type, Liverpool
Printed and bound in the UK

Contents

Foreword

by Richard Whiteley

Hello and welcome to this monster book of *Countdown* brainteasers. What a delight! Here are pages and pages of words and number games for you to indulge in to your heart's content.

This is a good old-fashioned puzzle book. Just like the television programme, there are no gimmicks or gizmos here – we're a computer free zone! All the games have been painstakingly worked out by Michael Wylie and Damian Eadie. Both (of course) are producers of *Countdown* and both former finalists – Michael way back in 1983, where he lost to Joyce Cansfield in Series 1, and Damian, a positive new boy, who triumphed in the final of Series 28 over Wayne Kelly in 1994.

People often call *Countdown* a quiz show but, in the strictest sense, it is not. There are no questions, merely a set of problems which require solutions. I like to call it a parlour game, in the great tradition of the programmes which were on the wireless when I was a child. Do you remember *Twenty Questions?* You had to guess an object with the help of just three clues – animal, vegetable or mineral. Or how about *Have a Go*, in which Wilfred Pickles and Mabel interviewed people in village halls all over the country? These programmes ran for years and millions tuned in.

The same can be said of television. We got a television set in 1952 (well before the Coronation which made us very posh!) and one of my earliest recollections is of tuning into *What's My Line.* A panel of four had to guess someone's job, helped only by a simple mime act. The programme ran for years in Britain and it is still broadcast in many places all over the world. All of these programmes – all based on simple concepts – have stood the test of time. And so, I think, has *Countdown.* It retains its original look (a look we thought was trendy in 1982 but now seems positively retro) and that is the beauty of it. We won't change anything just for the sake of it. We believe that is why many millions find the programme so addictive. And because we will never run out of words or numbers – there is no reason why *Countdown* shouldn't continue to run and run.

When we started out in November 1982, as the first programme on Channel 4's opening night, we had been given a five-week run. Who would have believed then that we would go on to clock up over 18 years and 3,000 programmes? In 2001 we are still going strong, with over 3.5 million viewers each day and a contract from Channel 4 until mid-2004!

For so many of us – young and old – *Countdown* at 4.30 in the afternoon has established itself as a fixed point in our daily timetable. It's an all too brief but reliable period in which to forget the hurly burly outside and exercise our brains. For every Granny and Granddad watching there is a grandson and granddaughter, which means we are constantly replenishing our audience as the years go on. And now that we have *Countdown* in a book, there's no need to wait until 4.30 for a daily fix!

Good luck. I warn you, these puzzles require some application and dedication. They're fun but not for the fainthearted. And if you do well and think you could have a bash at the real thing, well, who knows, we might meet up in the *Countdown* studio.

All the best,
Richard Whiteley

The rules of the game

In the programme, *Countdown* consists of 15 rounds – 11 letters games, 3 numbers games and a conundrum.

Letters games

- A contestant selects 9 letters from two piles of face-down cards (1 containing consonants, the other vowels).
- Each selection of 9 letters must contain either 3, 4 or 5 vowels, with the remainder being consonants. When the last letter has been selected, the clock is started and both contestants have 30 seconds to make the longest word they can from the letters available.
- Each letter may be used only once and only the longest word scores.
- Scoring: 1 point per letter, except for a 9-letter word – which earns 18 points.

Numbers games

- One contestant selects 6 numbers from 24 that are available. There are 4 rows to select from, the top row contains the numbers 25, 50, 75, 100; the other three rows contain the numbers 1–10 twice.
- A random 3-digit target from 100–999 is set and both contestants have 30 seconds to achieve this

target, using only the four basic disciplines of addition, subtraction, multiplication and division. (No powers, fractions or decimals etc.)

- Contestants may use any or all of the numbers but may use each number only once.
- Scoring the target exactly earns 10 points. Within 5 earns 7 points and within 10 gets 5 points. Any more than 10 away from the target fails to score.

Conundrums

- A board revolves to reveal a jumbled-up 9-letter word. The contestants have to guess this 9-letter word within 30 seconds. The round is on the buzzer, and the first contestant to answer correctly gets 10 points. If a contestant gives an incorrect answer then they are excluded from any further attempts at answering and the remainder of the time is given to their opponent.

How to use this book

Letters Games

Try and make the longest word you can by using the letters in the given selection. Each letter may only be used once and you should allow yourself just 30 seconds to play each round, but if you want to take longer then please yourself. You score 1 point per letter used but you get 18 points for a 9-letter word.

Proper nouns, hyphenated words and words with capital letters are not allowed. The answers are at the back of the book, and all words given are to be found in *Countdown*'s word bible – The New Oxford Dictionary of English.

Numbers Games

You are given 6 numbers to work with that are your tools to help you reach the given target. Use any or all of the numbers but only use each number once. Only addition, multiplication, subtraction and division are allowed and you must stick to whole numbers only at all stages of your calculations – no fractions !!

Conundrum

Find the hidden 9-letter word from the letters given. A correct answer scores 10 points. As a rule of thumb, we never use 8-letter plurals as conundrums – so words like TROMBONES will never appear. All conundrums should have only one answer – but if you happen to spot a legitimate alternative then it's 10 points to you – and a rotten egg to Michael Wylie!

Hints and tips for playing the *Countdown* games

Letters games

There is no quick guide to success when it comes to finding long words. Firstly, you must know of the word – otherwise you'll never find it in the first place, so nobody is ever going to find the longest in every single round.

For example, in a selection of A A I I R H K T S, most people would struggle to get any further than shark. However, there is a 9-letter word, TARAHIKIS (fish), but unless you know of it, you are never going to find it.

However, you can increase your chances of success by looking for typical word endings that are commonplace in the English language.

Words ending in –iest, –er, –ing, –ted, etc, can often be found in selections; and trying to find words constructed like this is always a good place to start. Likewise, words starting with over–, out–, re– are often tucked away in there too.

Also, depending upon the letters in the selection, it can often be fruitful to pair together letters that have natural partners and see what can be made. For example, C + K, C + H, P + L etc.

Another tip is to always look out for double letters that can go together. Pairing together o's, e's, d's, l's, etc can yield some king-sized words. Remember that the letter 'S' is a valuable bonus that can help to make plurals, which means longer words.

Lastly, the best advice of all is that you enjoy tackling the puzzles and try to beat your own personal targets. So if your highest word ever is a 7, strive for the 8 and then aim to repeat it. Once you think you have what it takes, write to us for an application form and then wait and see what happens.

Conundrums

Most people are of the opinion that you either see them straight away or you don't get them at all. This is not really the best way to look at a conundrum. If you can't see it in 2 seconds flat, then spend the next 28 reworking the selection to see if something comes up.

Look for the endings, look for conundrums that are made up of two smaller words, e.g. CHEWLATER. You might find the word wheel then realise that the letters trac are left, making cart. Then, hey presto, you have CARTWHEEL

ROUND 1

LETTER GAME 1

G	E	B	O	L	S	K	A	C

LETTER GAME 3

A	L	L	E	R	U	P	I	S

NUMBER GAME 1

25	6	8	3	7	7	860

CONUNDRUM

B	L	A	I	R	D	A	M	E

LETTER GAME 2

O	N	D	E	L	I	N	D	A

LETTER GAME 4

A	G	F	D	E	R	U	S	A

NUMBER GAME 2

50	8	9	2	2	4	**916**

SOLUTION

ROUND 2

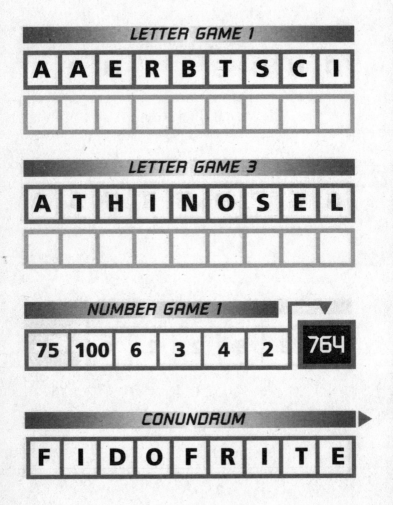

LETTER GAME 1

A	A	E	R	B	T	S	C	I

LETTER GAME 3

A	T	H	I	N	O	S	E	L

NUMBER GAME 1

75	100	6	3	4	2	764

CONUNDRUM

F	I	D	O	F	R	I	T	E

LETTER GAME 2

D	U	N	L	O	E	D	A	I

LETTER GAME 4

G	T	E	N	W	E	O	A	T

NUMBER GAME 2

100	5	10	9	1	1	469

SOLUTION

ROUND 3

LETTER GAME 1

A	A	E	T	I	R	N	J	K

LETTER GAME 3

G	E	S	U	T	A	P	D	A

NUMBER GAME 1

75	25	50	3	7	5	**914**

CONUNDRUM

S	I	G	M	A	S	N	A	G

LETTER GAME 2

L	I	B	E	K	S	O	H	J

LETTER GAME 4

S	S	E	E	D	I	R	C	L

NUMBER GAME 2

6	4	3	9	9	10	833

SOLUTION

ROUND 4

LETTER GAME 1

D	I	N	P	P	E	I	W	A

LETTER GAME 3

G	I	S	S	E	R	A	L	L

NUMBER GAME 1

50	25	100	75	8	6	486

CONUNDRUM

L	I	O	N	V	I	S	I	T

LETTER GAME 2

B	R	R	G	A	U	E	H	M

LETTER GAME 4

C	H	E	T	A	C	O	S	E

NUMBER GAME 2

25	2	4	4	5	3	**615**

SOLUTION

ROUND 5

LETTER GAME 1

A	N	T	I	D	O	T	E	S

LETTER GAME 3

H	E	R	C	A	R	S	O	E

NUMBER GAME 1

50	8	10	3	10	7	291

CONUNDRUM

T	E	D	C	A	R	T	E	R

LETTER GAME 2

C	A	N	I	C	A	T	E	V

LETTER GAME 4

A	A	D	V	R	E	Y	G	L

NUMBER GAME 2

50	75	6	5	6	7	522

SOLUTION

ROUND 6

LETTER GAME 1

A	D	E	E	N	K	H	R	T

LETTER GAME 3

C	L	I	N	U	A	Z	E	V

NUMBER GAME 1

25	2	9	8	4	3	**877**

CONUNDRUM

G	I	A	N	T	L	I	N	E

LETTER GAME 2

G	A	T	R	I	N	U	S	E

LETTER GAME 4

A	E	P	T	C	O	J	S	K

NUMBER GAME 2

100	25	50	8	5	6		347

SOLUTION

ROUND 7

LETTER GAME 1

A	A	B	C	R	E	M	D	T

LETTER GAME 3

S	U	S	I	T	R	A	C	Y

NUMBER GAME 1

75	9	6	9	8	3	777

CONUNDRUM

L	E	G	M	A	N	T	E	N

LETTER GAME 2

D	E	W	L	T	O	A	P	L

LETTER GAME 4

B	E	U	N	T	O	M	U	R

NUMBER GAME 2

2	5	6	10	3	2

474

SOLUTION

ROUND 8

LETTER GAME 1

K	E	N	A	G	W	I	N	O

LETTER GAME 3

M	U	S	T	I	E	M	Y	O

NUMBER GAME 1

25	9	4	1	3	1	**655**

CONUNDRUM

F	U	N	D	U	N	D	O	E

LETTER GAME 2

L	E	B	E	T	A	G	A	L

LETTER GAME 4

C	A	G	K	B	L	U	O	T

NUMBER GAME 2

100	8	7	10	2	2	**338**

SOLUTION

ROUND 9

LETTER GAME 1

U	P	U	N	L	O	R	A	P

LETTER GAME 3

P	E	S	C	Y	C	A	T	I

NUMBER GAME 1

50	100	5	8	8	4	**759**

CONUNDRUM

W	A	S	H	D	I	N	G	O

LETTER GAME 2

B	O	B	W	E	I	R	L	A

LETTER GAME 4

D	R	I	C	A	V	C	E	A

NUMBER GAME 2

75	25	1	10	7	6	**924**

SOLUTION

ROUND 10

LETTER GAME 1

D	Y	S	E	T	L	I	A	L

LETTER GAME 3

T	R	Y	A	D	O	I	N	E

NUMBER GAME 1

25	8	5	3	2	3

339

CONUNDRUM

S	T	R	A	P	T	O	R	N

LETTER GAME 2

M	N	M	T	E	R	O	A	E

LETTER GAME 4

R	D	E	M	T	A	P	E	H

NUMBER GAME 2

100	9	10	9	7	10	216

SOLUTION

ROUND 11

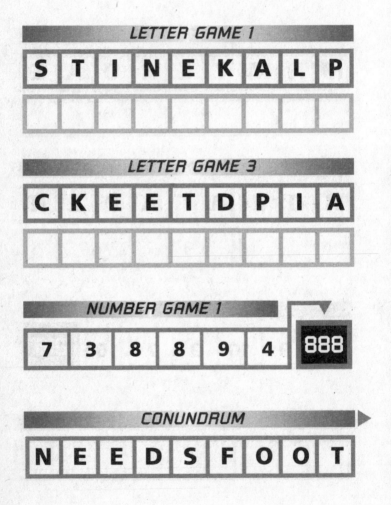

LETTER GAME 1

S	T	I	N	E	K	A	L	P

LETTER GAME 3

C	K	E	E	T	D	P	I	A

NUMBER GAME 1

7	3	8	8	9	4	888

CONUNDRUM

N	E	E	D	S	F	O	O	T

LETTER GAME 2

P	O	N	D	E	W	B	O	T

LETTER GAME 4

C	R	A	N	T	O	S	U	B

NUMBER GAME 2

50	75	100	25	5	5

740

SOLUTION

ROUND 12

LETTER GAME 1

A	A	D	R	R	E	H	W	I

LETTER GAME 3

Y	E	L	V	I	G	O	L	N

NUMBER GAME 1

25	50	4	8	10	8	**173**

CONUNDRUM

D	I	R	G	E	L	A	N	D

LETTER GAME 2

H	E	R	M	P	A	S	I	F

LETTER GAME 4

B	A	D	D	A	Y	R	I	R

NUMBER GAME 2

100	9	1	2	3	4		671

SOLUTION

ROUND 13

LETTER GAME 1

Z	C	D	E	N	A	A	K	F

LETTER GAME 3

Y	E	T	B	I	O	L	K	R

NUMBER GAME 1

75	6	10	3	3	8	**856**

CONUNDRUM

I	T	S	A	L	O	O	N	I

LETTER GAME 2

K	E	G	I	N	T	R	A	C

LETTER GAME 4

N	Z	I	E	M	W	A	O	D

NUMBER GAME 2

50	75	100	9	7	6	**461**

SOLUTION

ROUND 14

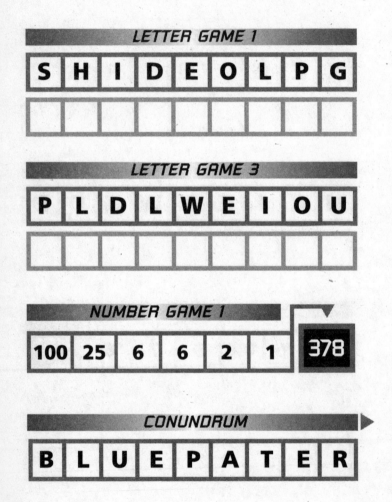

LETTER GAME 1

S	H	I	D	E	O	L	P	G

LETTER GAME 3

P	L	D	L	W	E	I	O	U

NUMBER GAME 1

100	25	6	6	2	1	378

CONUNDRUM

B	L	U	E	P	A	T	E	R

LETTER GAME 2

R	E	D	V	I	L	E	D	A

LETTER GAME 4

M	L	I	B	A	N	E	T	P

NUMBER GAME 2

25	4	10	7	1	9	**883**

SOLUTION

ROUND 15

LETTER GAME 1

D	T	R	U	N	E	L	A	E

LETTER GAME 3

M	I	L	A	C	A	Y	T	U

NUMBER GAME 1

75	100	4	2	2	5	662

CONUNDRUM

R	I	F	L	E	D	E	C	K

LETTER GAME 2

G	N	E	P	T	R	I	A	D

LETTER GAME 4

F	U	G	N	T	H	I	B	O

NUMBER GAME 2

25	100	75	3	2	4	823

SOLUTION

47

ROUND 16

LETTER GAME 1

A	R	O	I	T	A	D	R	Y

LETTER GAME 3

C	U	S	P	N	E	A	E	G

NUMBER GAME 1

50	75	6	8	1	2	557

CONUNDRUM

G	I	A	N	T	T	O	O	T

LETTER GAME 2

N	E	X	I	S	C	P	E	R

LETTER GAME 4

A	S	C	I	L	E	M	F	I

NUMBER GAME 2

25	3	5	6	7	1	**991**

SOLUTION

ROUND 17

LETTER GAME 1

A	A	D	G	O	P	S	E	K

LETTER GAME 3

G	R	U	S	T	O	R	E	A

NUMBER GAME 1

75	50	6	2	1	8	674

CONUNDRUM

S	H	O	U	T	W	H	A	M

LETTER GAME 2

M	M	I	H	O	S	C	A	E

LETTER GAME 4

S	C	M	N	E	I	A	L	U

NUMBER GAME 2

100	10	5	2	3	2	857

SOLUTION

ROUND 18

LETTER GAME 1

B	R	R	O	T	A	A	D	D

LETTER GAME 3

D	R	G	M	E	I	T	A	E

NUMBER GAME 1

3	7	4	4	9	9	**536**

CONUNDRUM

A	F	R	E	E	L	I	F	T

LETTER GAME 2

G	E	L	I	N	I	D	Y	O

LETTER GAME 4

G	I	R	S	E	V	A	T	H

NUMBER GAME 2

25	1	2	10	9	2	**779**

SOLUTION

ROUND 19

LETTER GAME 1

R	O	S	E	I	M	W	O	R

LETTER GAME 3

D	E	R	B	O	W	A	R	I

NUMBER GAME 1

50	4	3	7	1	5	**963**

CONUNDRUM

B	E	R	L	I	N	M	U	G

LETTER GAME 2

E	B	I	J	R	A	L	K	A

LETTER GAME 4

L	L	B	E	I	A	S	T	O

NUMBER GAME 2

100	75	25	50	7	10	618

SOLUTION

ROUND 20

LETTER GAME 1

A	N	A	T	I	R	O	C	K

LETTER GAME 3

F	H	A	M	S	T	A	E	C

NUMBER GAME 1

25	100	4	1	2	7	**860**

CONUNDRUM

N	A	G	S	H	R	I	E	K

LETTER GAME 2

G	U	L	I	B	I	N	A	L

LETTER GAME 4

T	R	A	B	E	G	U	D	Y

NUMBER GAME 2

75	6	5	10	10	3	**864**

75 * 10 * 10 = 850   6+5+3 = 14
= 85   850+14 = 864

SOLUTION

ROUND 21

LETTER GAME 1

F	L	O	D	E	C	A	B	O

LETTER GAME 3

A	D	E	E	R	O	W	V	T

NUMBER GAME 1

75	100	6	9	9	7	**337**

CONUNDRUM

R	I	G	C	O	R	D	O	N

LETTER GAME 2

S	N	O	P	S	E	T	S	I

LETTER GAME 4

D	O	L	S	I	P	O	E	L

NUMBER GAME 2

50	2	8	8	9	1	**683**

SOLUTION

ROUND 22

LETTER GAME 1

A	R	B	C	I	U	B	Y	A

LETTER GAME 3

G	U	N	Y	S	O	T	E	I

NUMBER GAME 1

25	50	100	5	4	8	**916**

CONUNDRUM

N	I	C	K	T	E	S	S	A

LETTER GAME 2

A	A	S	E	T	B	D	A	R

LETTER GAME 4

A	I	P	L	L	N	O	T	B

NUMBER GAME 2

75	4	2	2	1	6	**573**

SOLUTION

ROUND 23

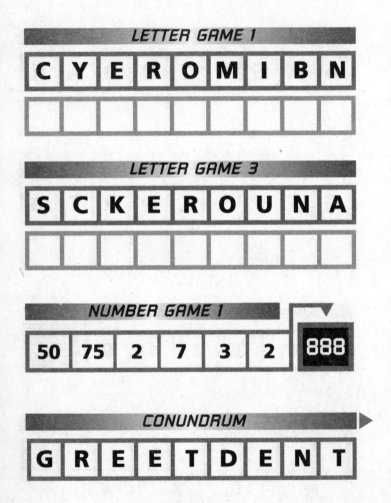

LETTER GAME 1

C	Y	E	R	O	M	I	B	N

LETTER GAME 3

S	C	K	E	R	O	U	N	A

NUMBER GAME 1

50	75	2	7	3	2	888

CONUNDRUM

G	R	E	E	T	D	E	N	T

LETTER GAME 2

G	U	R	I	N	C	A	N	I

LETTER GAME 4

G	E	N	T	R	I	A	T	G

NUMBER GAME 2

100	50	75	25	10	9

204

SOLUTION

ROUND 24

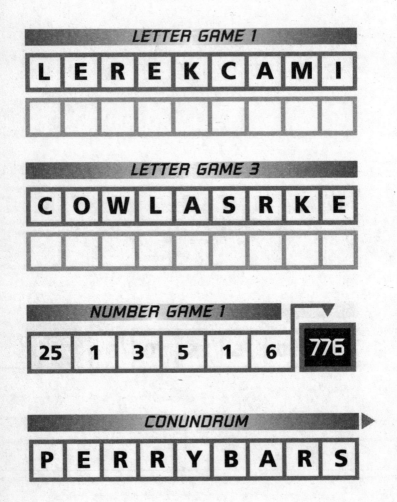

LETTER GAME 1

L	E	R	E	K	C	A	M	I

LETTER GAME 3

C	O	W	L	A	S	R	K	E

NUMBER GAME 1

25	1	3	5	1	6	**776**

CONUNDRUM

P	E	R	R	Y	B	A	R	S

LETTER GAME 2

M	I	D	H	E	A	S	F	O

LETTER GAME 4

M	O	N	O	D	E	A	L	P

NUMBER GAME 2

3	10	7	4	4	5	635

SOLUTION

ROUND 25

LETTER GAME 1

J	U	D	E	L	T	A	N	S

LETTER GAME 3

A	B	E	C	I	L	A	N	T

NUMBER GAME 1

75	25	4	4	7	2	**966**

CONUNDRUM

D	I	V	O	T	M	E	A	T

LETTER GAME 2

G	E	N	V	E	A	S	C	Y

LETTER GAME 4

G	I	N	J	E	A	S	L	T

NUMBER GAME 2

8	5	5	7	2	1	642

SOLUTION

ROUND 26

LETTER GAME 1

A	E	F	L	P	R	Y	E	S

LETTER GAME 3

C	L	O	B	I	S	E	A	N

NUMBER GAME 1

100	10	9	10	1	7	**741**

CONUNDRUM

P	I	N	C	H	G	E	A	R

LETTER GAME 2

C	C	A	R	I	O	N	T	I

LETTER GAME 4

A	D	I	I	O	N	S	B	E

NUMBER GAME 2

50	8	6	9	1	2	**656**

SOLUTION

ROUND 27

LETTER GAME 1

T	H	O	R	E	B	R	U	A

LETTER GAME 3

S	E	P	X	D	I	A	Z	C

NUMBER GAME 1

25	50	100	75	1	9

522

CONUNDRUM

N	I	E	C	E	T	I	F	F

LETTER GAME 2

T	S	I	N	E	R	G	A	V

LETTER GAME 4

A	B	E	L	I	Z	E	S	D

NUMBER GAME 2

75	6	5	8	3	1	**999**

SOLUTION

ROUND 28

LETTER GAME 1

D	O	L	O	V	I	A	N	T

LETTER GAME 3

S	T	E	A	S	I	T	E	Z

NUMBER GAME 1

25	50	2	5	5	10	723

CONUNDRUM

S	O	L	A	R	B	A	T	S

LETTER GAME 2

A	D	E	E	G	H	R	A	X

LETTER GAME 4

A	R	G	T	R	A	N	O	E

NUMBER GAME 2

100	9	10	5	3	3	**648**

SOLUTION

ROUND 29

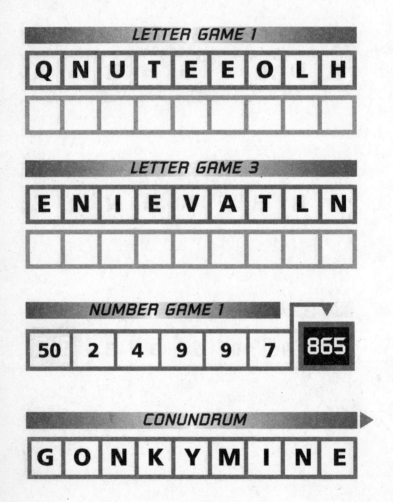

LETTER GAME 1

Q	N	U	T	E	E	O	L	H

LETTER GAME 3

E	N	I	E	V	A	T	L	N

NUMBER GAME 1

50	2	4	9	9	7	865

CONUNDRUM

G	O	N	K	Y	M	I	N	E

LETTER GAME 2

Z	I	D	C	O	H	I	S	E

LETTER GAME 4

D	E	T	I	P	O	N	A	C

NUMBER GAME 2

75	50	100	10	4	6	787

SOLUTION

ROUND 30

LETTER GAME 1

A	R	T	R	I	P	O	T	E

LETTER GAME 3

T	O	E	L	I	S	T	T	H

NUMBER GAME 1

100	8	5	1	4	9	234

CONUNDRUM

A	M	A	D	N	U	D	G	E

LETTER GAME 2

A	A	G	E	M	I	N	Z	D

LETTER GAME 4

C	H	O	B	R	I	E	S	T

NUMBER GAME 2

25	4	3	2	1	1	**431**

SOLUTION

ROUND 31

LETTER GAME 1

| C | R | E | N | S | U | W | A | A |

LETTER GAME 3

| L | I | V | E | N | S | J | A | Y |

NUMBER GAME 1

| 50 | 100 | 8 | 4 | 9 | 4 | **677** |

CONUNDRUM

| P | I | E | R | C | E | N | O | T |

LETTER GAME 2

B	R	E	D	A	W	T	E	I

LETTER GAME 4

A	P	E	T	E	R	R	A	Y

NUMBER GAME 2

75	5	8	4	8	3	**945**

SOLUTION

ROUND 32

LETTER GAME 1

D	E	L	I	B	U	M	C	N

LETTER GAME 3

D	E	N	U	T	N	A	W	G

NUMBER GAME 1

100	7	6	1	2	7	880

CONUNDRUM

A	S	E	M	I	S	P	I	V

LETTER GAME 2

C	I	D	L	A	R	H	E	T

LETTER GAME 4

C	L	E	S	A	B	E	G	D

NUMBER GAME 2

25	75	100	6	5	9	**724**

SOLUTION

ROUND 33

LETTER GAME 1

A	N	R	W	S	T	O	R	E

LETTER GAME 3

T	I	V	E	P	A	T	A	C

NUMBER GAME 1

8	3	9	9	7	8	**906**

CONUNDRUM

D	E	N	T	R	E	I	G	N

LETTER GAME 2

A	C	D	E	I	M	P	N	O

LETTER GAME 4

H	P	E	N	T	A	L	E	D

NUMBER GAME 2

50	4	4	7	5	5		639

SOLUTION

ROUND 34

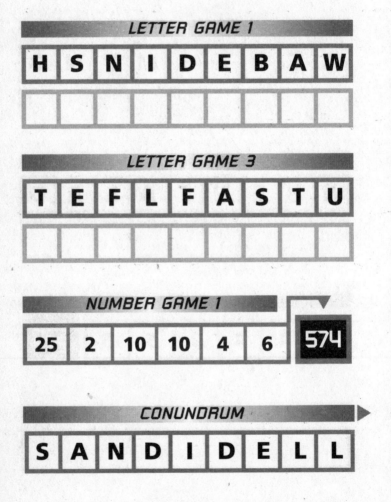

LETTER GAME 1

H	S	N	I	D	E	B	A	W

LETTER GAME 3

T	E	F	L	F	A	S	T	U

NUMBER GAME 1

25	2	10	10	4	6	**574**

CONUNDRUM

S	A	N	D	I	D	E	L	L

LETTER GAME 2

D	E	R	E	S	O	T	V	E

LETTER GAME 4

W	L	L	E	E	R	F	A	I

NUMBER GAME 2

75	100	5	3	3	7	**955**

SOLUTION

ROUND 35

LETTER GAME 1

P	R	O	N	O	I	C	S	O

LETTER GAME 3

M	E	X	I	L	O	B	A	S

NUMBER GAME 1

100	75	50	25	8	8	**620**

CONUNDRUM

A	S	U	G	A	R	S	A	P

LETTER GAME 2

F	R	E	I	B	A	S	E	C

LETTER GAME 4

M	M	A	R	C	D	O	A	E

NUMBER GAME 2

25	2	10	3	9	4	785

SOLUTION

ROUND 36

LETTER GAME 1

X	C	L	W	A	T	H	O	E

LETTER GAME 3

B	P	O	U	F	M	I	Z	Y

NUMBER GAME 1

50	25	10	9	9	2

814

CONUNDRUM

M	O	O	W	H	E	E	L	S

LETTER GAME 2

D	E	H	I	W	A	R	V	C

LETTER GAME 4

A	T	I	C	E	M	E	T	D

NUMBER GAME 2

75	100	50	6	9	9	**249**

SOLUTION

89

ROUND 37

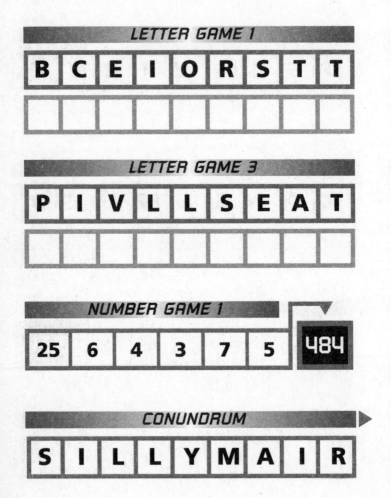

LETTER GAME 1

B	C	E	I	O	R	S	T	T

LETTER GAME 3

P	I	V	L	L	S	E	A	T

NUMBER GAME 1

25	6	4	3	7	5	**484**

CONUNDRUM

S	I	L	L	Y	M	A	I	R

LETTER GAME 2

R	E	I	P	D	N	A	G	N

LETTER GAME 4

D	X	Y	M	I	R	T	E	A

NUMBER GAME 2

50	25	100	8	2	7	**530**

SOLUTION

ROUND 38

LETTER GAME 1

L	N	S	E	R	I	C	E	A

LETTER GAME 3

S	T	E	X	A	L	Y	H	E

NUMBER GAME 1

6	8	10	1	9	2	**516**

CONUNDRUM

P	U	L	L	E	T	M	I	X

LETTER GAME 2

D	R	U	S	T	O	P	E	G

LETTER GAME 4

D	H	K	I	S	E	A	N	R

NUMBER GAME 2

75	100	25	3	4	9	**702**

SOLUTION

ROUND 39

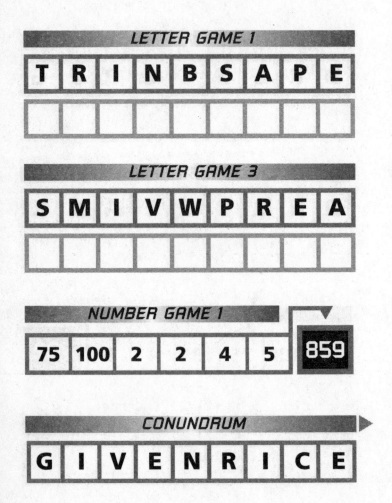

LETTER GAME 1

T	R	I	N	B	S	A	P	E

LETTER GAME 3

S	M	I	V	W	P	R	E	A

NUMBER GAME 1

75	100	2	2	4	5	**859**

CONUNDRUM

G	I	V	E	N	R	I	C	E

LETTER GAME 2

C	P	L	U	L	E	U	K	E

LETTER GAME 4

N	N	A	D	K	I	G	E	W

NUMBER GAME 2

50	25	75	100	3	6	**427**

SOLUTION

ROUND 40

LETTER GAME 1

H	B	K	S	A	C	A	I	C

LETTER GAME 3

S	U	R	I	P	D	E	A	T

NUMBER GAME 1

50	9	9	6	3	4	**731**

CONUNDRUM

T	O	Y	R	I	P	P	E	R

LETTER GAME 2

A	N	S	N	S	T	E	S	I

LETTER GAME 4

G	R	E	B	I	T	A	N	N

NUMBER GAME 2

25	6	10	3	2	2	**990**

SOLUTION

ROUND 41

LETTER GAME 1

A	E	E	K	V	O	R	M	D

LETTER GAME 3

B	L	R	C	W	E	A	L	S

NUMBER GAME 1

50	5	7	9	3	4	**870**

CONUNDRUM

W	A	N	D	A	S	B	I	T

LETTER GAME 2

P	T	C	R	E	E	D	I	H

LETTER GAME 4

C	I	T	K	S	O	T	S	E

NUMBER GAME 2

25	50	100	6	9	2	**393**

SOLUTION

ROUND 42

LETTER GAME 1

F	E	R	I	C	A	S	E	E

LETTER GAME 3

I	L	I	S	T	E	R	A	C

NUMBER GAME 1

9	6	4	4	5	5	**721**

CONUNDRUM

L	E	E	B	R	O	P	H	Y

LETTER GAME 2

M	A	T	U	T	I	E	L	G

LETTER GAME 4

S	E	R	T	O	L	A	M	E

NUMBER GAME 2

5	6	7	1	2	3	840

SOLUTION

ROUND 43

LETTER GAME 1

| L | A | V | I | G | E | R | L | O |

LETTER GAME 3

| T | H | U | C | N | L | Y | O | U |

NUMBER GAME 1

| 25 | 8 | 9 | 3 | 2 | 3 |

654

CONUNDRUM

| A | S | O | U | R | B | O | I | L |

LETTER GAME 2

F	R	E	D	B	A	T	E	S

LETTER GAME 4

A	D	N	N	C	I	H	R	E

NUMBER GAME 2

100	75	8	9	10	7	**369**

SOLUTION

ROUND 44

LETTER GAME 1

E	L	L	I	S	T	A	C	E

LETTER GAME 3

F	C	D	E	R	U	A	S	T

NUMBER GAME 1

50	2	3	1	7	2	992

CONUNDRUM

T	E	A	C	O	F	F	I	N

LETTER GAME 2

A	R	C	H	A	P	T	E	U

LETTER GAME 4

H	A	R	F	I	N	G	T	G

NUMBER GAME 2

25	100	4	6	8	4	**757**

SOLUTION

ROUND 45

LETTER GAME 1

A	A	C	I	O	R	N	S	F

LETTER GAME 3

C	A	R	E	I	P	S	T	O

NUMBER GAME 1

100	25	75	50	10	1	**393**

CONUNDRUM

L	O	N	G	N	O	I	S	E

LETTER GAME 2

A	G	N	E	E	R	I	D	T

LETTER GAME 4

S	O	C	N	O	T	P	A	E

NUMBER GAME 2

25	75	50	4	9	8	**894**

SOLUTION

ROUND 46

LETTER GAME 1

O	O	M	R	J	E	A	B	T

LETTER GAME 3

R	H	D	I	G	A	N	C	E

NUMBER GAME 1

50	7	3	2	8	4	**924**

CONUNDRUM

V	I	E	W	A	B	A	R	N

LETTER GAME 2

C	H	M	O	D	E	A	T	S

LETTER GAME 4

G	U	F	I	L	O	T	S	O

NUMBER GAME 2

50	75	9	8	10	4	**529**

SOLUTION

ROUND 47

LETTER GAME 1

E	N	B	E	R	I	D	L	A

LETTER GAME 3

S	F	Y	L	U	M	E	I	H

NUMBER GAME 1

100	1	6	5	1	7	**837**

CONUNDRUM

F	E	E	T	C	R	I	M	P

LETTER GAME 2

E	E	D	O	N	Y	W	H	A

LETTER GAME 4

F	R	E	D	B	E	C	A	A

NUMBER GAME 2

25	9	2	2	4	4	**671**

SOLUTION

ROUND 48

LETTER GAME 1

U	T	E	R	I	S	Y	T	A

LETTER GAME 3

C	R	I	P	V	O	E	R	E

NUMBER GAME 1

25	1	5	6	4	1	783

CONUNDRUM

G	R	E	A	T	M	I	N	K

LETTER GAME 2

S	B	A	Y	T	I	B	O	G

LETTER GAME 4

P	E	R	I	S	O	U	G	Y

NUMBER GAME 2

50	100	7	8	5	10	**624**

SOLUTION

ROUND 49

LETTER GAME 1

S	P	I	M	A	R	T	A	O

LETTER GAME 3

M	O	L	L	A	T	E	R	S

NUMBER GAME 1

75	2	3	9	1	6	**548**

CONUNDRUM

N	E	I	G	H	D	E	T	T

LETTER GAME 2

S	A	P	A	N	I	E	G	O

LETTER GAME 4

A	A	B	C	L	I	T	E	R

NUMBER GAME 2

100	75	25	50	4	6	**826**

SOLUTION

ROUND 50

LETTER GAME 1

B	U	D	O	N	E	W	S	T

LETTER GAME 3

B	R	E	D	H	E	A	S	A

NUMBER GAME 1

50	5	8	9	1	2	**633**

CONUNDRUM

C	R	O	O	L	C	E	L	T

LETTER GAME 2

T	O	L	E	Z	A	R	Y	E

LETTER GAME 4

W	I	T	R	E	L	L	A	S

NUMBER GAME 2

25	100	7	9	8	7	**444**

SOLUTION

ROUND 51

LETTER GAME 1

M	O	S	U	I	R	Q	E	D

LETTER GAME 3

B	R	Y	G	E	B	I	N	A

NUMBER GAME 1

50	100	25	9	9	2	**786**

CONUNDRUM

T	U	N	I	N	G	B	O	T

LETTER GAME 2

P	R	E	N	C	A	R	T	E

LETTER GAME 4

K	R	O	Y	B	E	A	O	T

NUMBER GAME 2

50	1	2	1	2	10	**676**

SOLUTION

ROUND 52

LETTER GAME 1

T	R	E	D	E	I	T	Y	X

LETTER GAME 3

T	O	R	K	I	P	A	N	W

NUMBER GAME 1

25	4	7	10	1	8	**555**

CONUNDRUM

S	P	L	I	C	E	D	A	D

LETTER GAME 2

C	L	I	M	O	R	A	T	A

LETTER GAME 4

L	U	C	H	E	Q	S	Y	I

NUMBER GAME 2

6	7	8	9	10	5	**744**

SOLUTION

ROUND 53

LETTER GAME 1

H	O	F	R	L	A	D	Y	O

LETTER GAME 3

F	Y	P	T	E	C	E	A	R

NUMBER GAME 1

25	50	75	100	8	3

687

CONUNDRUM

P	E	R	T	P	R	O	U	D

LETTER GAME 2

A	G	C	I	L	A	R	T	E

LETTER GAME 4

T	H	O	W	E	R	A	L	E

NUMBER GAME 2

25	4	7	8	5	9	**876**

SOLUTION

ROUND 54

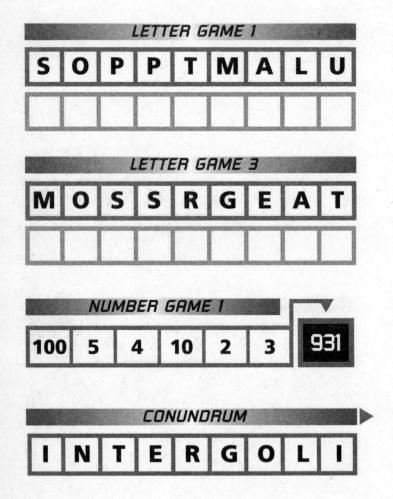

LETTER GAME 1

S	O	P	P	T	M	A	L	U

LETTER GAME 3

M	O	S	S	R	G	E	A	T

NUMBER GAME 1

100	5	4	10	2	3	931

CONUNDRUM

I	N	T	E	R	G	O	L	I

LETTER GAME 2

K	N	I	M	E	W	E	R	A

LETTER GAME 4

H	I	N	D	A	R	C	A	T

NUMBER GAME 2

50	25	75	3	1	2	**693**

SOLUTION

ROUND 55

LETTER GAME 1

D	E	R	P	I	N	A	G	S

LETTER GAME 3

H	U	R	P	I	D	M	T	E

NUMBER GAME 1

75	50	5	9	2	2	**988**

CONUNDRUM

M	O	T	H	L	I	C	K	S

LETTER GAME 2

| P | L | A | I | S | H | O | T | A |

| | | | | | | | | |

LETTER GAME 4

| K | C | E | E | R | A | T | A | R |

| | | | | | | | | |

NUMBER GAME 2

| 50 | 8 | 8 | 4 | 5 | 6 | **772** |

SOLUTION

| | | | | | | | | |

ROUND 56

LETTER GAME 1

S	R	E	A	M	T	B	E	W

LETTER GAME 3

L	A	R	N	A	B	C	E	T

NUMBER GAME 1

100	75	25	6	4	9	**840**

CONUNDRUM

N	I	M	B	L	G	E	R	T

LETTER GAME 2

C	I	F	C	E	I	P	S	T

LETTER GAME 4

S	A	W	A	L	I	D	E	S

NUMBER GAME 2

25	7	3	4	1	2	**366**

SOLUTION

ROUND 57

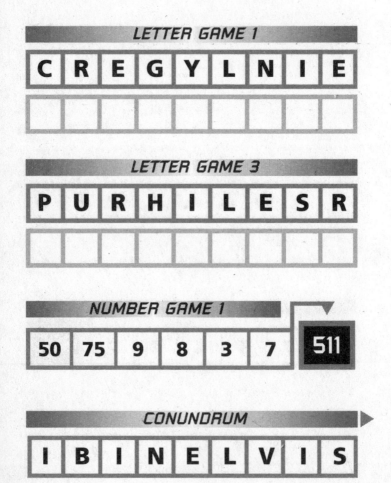

LETTER GAME 1

C	R	E	G	Y	L	N	I	E

LETTER GAME 3

P	U	R	H	I	L	E	S	R

NUMBER GAME 1

50	75	9	8	3	7	**511**

CONUNDRUM

I	B	I	N	E	L	V	I	S

LETTER GAME 2

L	U	B	L	I	N	E	T	S

LETTER GAME 4

S	P	E	C	A	K	N	A	M

NUMBER GAME 2

4	7	10	4	5	5	**835**

SOLUTION

ROUND 58

LETTER GAME 1

M	I	L	I	T	E	F	X	E

LETTER GAME 3

L	I	M	U	S	T	A	T	E

NUMBER GAME 1

75	4	8	9	10	9	**929**

CONUNDRUM

D	I	E	S	E	L	R	O	D

LETTER GAME 2

T	T	N	M	E	T	R	A	E

LETTER GAME 4

W	O	M	T	E	R	L	O	S

NUMBER GAME 2

25	75	100	3	7	8	**743**

SOLUTION

ROUND 59

LETTER GAME 1

R	O	P	E	R	A	W	S	H

LETTER GAME 3

S	H	U	W	E	R	O	A	E

NUMBER GAME 1

25	6	2	3	2	4	**854**

CONUNDRUM

S	I	M	I	A	N	T	O	Y

LETTER GAME 2

D	E	T	R	O	V	E	X	A

LETTER GAME 4

P	N	CH	H	R	O	E	D	A

NUMBER GAME 2

25	100	50	75	10	10		306

SOLUTION

ROUND 60

LETTER GAME 1

C	O	R	O	T	A	M	D	E

LETTER GAME 3

Z	E	C	T	I	R	U	E	A

NUMBER GAME 1

75	8	4	5	10	8	**933**

CONUNDRUM

I	R	A	N	D	I	N	G	O

LETTER GAME 2

C	O	N	P	U	S	O	K	C

LETTER GAME 4

L	I	N	P	L	O	T	A	B

NUMBER GAME 2

100	50	7	9	8	9	521

SOLUTION

ROUND 61

LETTER GAME 1

P	E	R	S	T	I	R	N	A

LETTER GAME 3

S	U	U	L	T	R	E	V	I

NUMBER GAME 1

25	5	8	10	5	3	414

CONUNDRUM

H	I	T	A	B	B	E	S	S

LETTER GAME 2

U	M	O	S	E	T	A	L	P

LETTER GAME 4

X	I	D	E	F	O	Y	T	C

NUMBER GAME 2

2	7	10	3	4	4

672

SOLUTION

ROUND 62

LETTER GAME 1

O	C	T	U	S	E	P	L	R

LETTER GAME 3

G	O	N	I	L	A	H	O	W

NUMBER GAME 1

50	5	10	2	2	4	**967**

CONUNDRUM

D	D	E	E	R	H	U	N	T

LETTER GAME 2

Q	E	N	T	A	B	U	D	E

LETTER GAME 4

G	A	R	D	I	P	A	L	E

NUMBER GAME 2

75	100	6	1	7	5	**859**

SOLUTION

ROUND 63

LETTER GAME 1

G	U	R	Y	V	E	O	A	F

LETTER GAME 3

R	O	E	L	I	S	T	E	T

NUMBER GAME 1

50	3	4	2	9	9	**999**

CONUNDRUM

R	O	C	S	W	R	E	C	K

LETTER GAME 2

D	R	O	B	E	L	I	A	P

LETTER GAME 4

R	E	M	O	R	B	O	S	T

NUMBER GAME 2

25	100	75	50	6	8	**222**

SOLUTION

ROUND 64

LETTER GAME 1

F	O	T	E	K	A	C	B	S

LETTER GAME 3

D	A	M	E	R	T	A	S	N

NUMBER GAME 1

100	75	5	3	7	7	**616**

CONUNDRUM

G	I	N	P	O	T	T	I	E

LETTER GAME 2

S	Q	U	E	R	P	A	T	D

LETTER GAME 4

P	H	E	R	I	M	O	N	K

NUMBER GAME 2

25	2	3	4	1	4		619

SOLUTION

ROUND 65

LETTER GAME 1

Q	I	B	E	U	T	S	R	O

LETTER GAME 3

B	E	N	I	S	R	A	C	K

NUMBER GAME 1

50	10	5	4	3	7	876

CONUNDRUM

T	E	A	B	R	E	A	T	H

LETTER GAME 2

I	V	E	L	I	M	O	C	A

LETTER GAME 4

M	O	N	G	I	L	A	F	P

NUMBER GAME 2

8	5	3	1	4	2	**522**

SOLUTION

ROUND 66

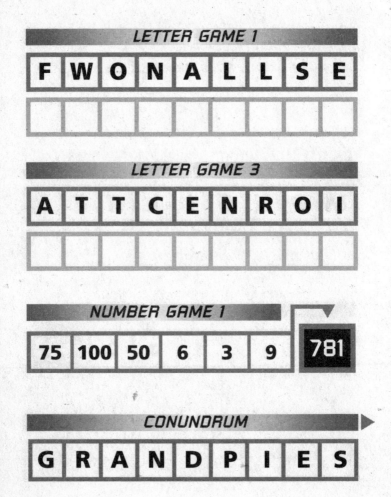

LETTER GAME 1

| F | W | O | N | A | L | L | S | E |

LETTER GAME 3

| A | T | T | C | E | N | R | O | I |

NUMBER GAME 1

| 75 | 100 | 50 | 6 | 3 | 9 | 781 |

CONUNDRUM

| G | R | A | N | D | P | I | E | S |

LETTER GAME 2

G	R	L	A	B	E	P	O	E

LETTER GAME 4

W	E	L	I	N	G	T	O	N

NUMBER GAME 2

100	10	9	1	2	2		933

SOLUTION

ROUND 67

LETTER GAME 1

S	O	N	O	C	A	M	P	E

LETTER GAME 3

K	O	R	E	S	O	N	O	L

NUMBER GAME 1

50	75	4	6	5	3	802

CONUNDRUM

S	I	M	M	E	R	S	E	E

LETTER GAME 2

H	I	G	N	O	L	R	A	W

LETTER GAME 4

G	U	N	I	L	T	O	V	A

NUMBER GAME 2

25	8	2	3	10	7	645

SOLUTION

ROUND 68

LETTER GAME 1

O	R	N	O	D	E	T	A	S

LETTER GAME 3

T	E	R	I	N	C	A	Y	T

NUMBER GAME 1

100	50	75	25	4	10	**283**

CONUNDRUM

S	U	P	E	R	D	E	A	D

LETTER GAME 2

L	I	R	G	A	N	S	N	O

LETTER GAME 4

S	T	A	L	I	Y	O	R	T

NUMBER GAME 2

75	2	4	3	1	2	**960**

SOLUTION

ROUND 69

LETTER GAME 1

S	O	D	E	P	L	A	E	B

LETTER GAME 3

S	P	U	I	N	B	E	S	M

NUMBER GAME 1

25	3	9	6	5	6	**611**

CONUNDRUM

C	A	S	E	D	T	H	I	S

LETTER GAME 2

H	O	M	O	D	E	C	S	I

LETTER GAME 4

M	E	R	N	U	A	S	E	Y

NUMBER GAME 2

50	25	10	4	8	3

319

SOLUTION

ROUND 70

LETTER GAME 1

S	I	N	C	U	A	S	E	R

LETTER GAME 3

T	E	D	I	S	P	U	C	A

NUMBER GAME 1

10	7	9	7	8	10	**621**

CONUNDRUM

S	U	P	E	R	D	O	O	N

LETTER GAME 2

D	R	N	E	W	A	N	D	E

LETTER GAME 4

L	U	T	O	M	A	D	E	Q

NUMBER GAME 2

25	50	9	4	3	2	**998**

SOLUTION

ROUND 71

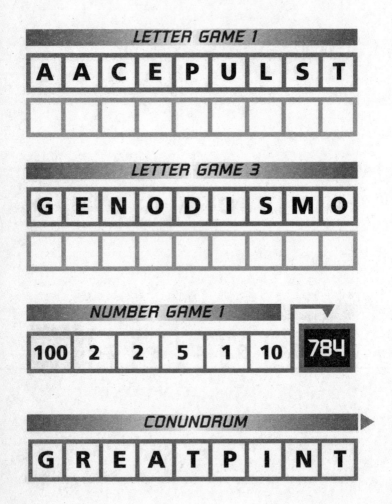

LETTER GAME 1

A	A	C	E	P	U	L	S	T

LETTER GAME 3

G	E	N	O	D	I	S	M	O

NUMBER GAME 1

100	2	2	5	1	10	**784**

CONUNDRUM

G	R	E	A	T	P	I	N	T

LETTER GAME 2

O	K	A	P	E	B	O	E	X

LETTER GAME 4

F	I	D	N	E	L	I	M	E

NUMBER GAME 2

25	10	7	9	9	2	**931**

SOLUTION

ROUND 72

LETTER GAME 1

B	R	I	N	T	E	A	H	E

LETTER GAME 3

R	R	R	I	S	B	T	E	A

NUMBER GAME 1

25	75	100	1	3	1	**882**

CONUNDRUM

L	O	C	A	L	D	A	T	E

LETTER GAME 2

B	L	U	N	I	M	A	T	H

LETTER GAME 4

O	L	D	E	D	B	A	T	P

NUMBER GAME 2

75	50	100	6	2	9	421

SOLUTION

ROUND 73

LETTER GAME 1

L	E	S	P	I	A	N	E	C

LETTER GAME 3

P	H	O	M	I	N	C	A	W

NUMBER GAME 1

75	8	6	10	2	4		**999**

CONUNDRUM

B	L	E	E	D	T	A	N	K

LETTER GAME 2

I	N	G	A	H	I	T	Y	N

LETTER GAME 4

H	O	P	I	N	E	R	W	S

NUMBER GAME 2

50	10	9	2	3	1	706

SOLUTION

ROUND 74

LETTER GAME 1

Z	A	I	D	L	V	R	O	S

LETTER GAME 3

W	I	N	E	V	A	R	B	A

NUMBER GAME 1

8	3	10	7	6	1	**909**

CONUNDRUM

I	N	T	O	M	A	N	I	A

LETTER GAME 2

D	E	N	H	O	M	A	T	E

LETTER GAME 4

T	I	A	L	P	O	C	S	W

NUMBER GAME 2

50	100	4	3	1	8	**634**

SOLUTION

ROUND 75

LETTER GAME 1

T	H	U	P	O	N	S	E	E

LETTER GAME 3

H	O	M	O	B	R	A	T	W

NUMBER GAME 1

25	50	75	10	10	9	**377**

CONUNDRUM

I	B	I	T	E	H	A	N	D

LETTER GAME 2

F	C	L	U	N	K	F	I	A

LETTER GAME 4

B	U	D	R	A	N	I	S	E

NUMBER GAME 2

25	7	9	9	4	3	**858**

SOLUTION

ROUND 76

LETTER GAME 1

L	A	T	E	S	E	L	K	O

LETTER GAME 3

M	T	R	E	I	C	O	S	I

NUMBER GAME 1

25	100	6	4	5	2	**880**

CONUNDRUM

S	U	G	A	R	I	C	O	N

LETTER GAME 2

Y	T	H	I	M	A	N	G	E

LETTER GAME 4

Y	T	N	O	B	E	A	D	E

NUMBER GAME 2

75	2	10	10	5	7	**468**

SOLUTION

ROUND 77

LETTER GAME 1

H	V	C	O	N	A	I	S	E

LETTER GAME 3

C	I	R	E	N	S	T	I	Y

NUMBER GAME 1

50	100	4	5	4	5	**685**

CONUNDRUM

S	T	R	A	Y	M	O	O	N

LETTER GAME 2

A	C	D	E	E	I	L	U	T

LETTER GAME 4

M	R	U	O	S	I	N	G	O

NUMBER GAME 2

75	5	1	7	3	5	**666**

SOLUTION

ROUND 78

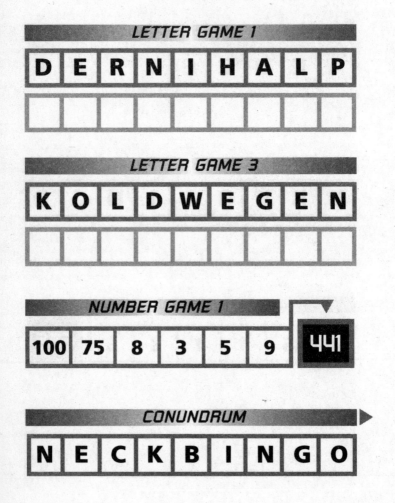

LETTER GAME 1

D	E	R	N	I	H	A	L	P

LETTER GAME 3

K	O	L	D	W	E	G	E	N

NUMBER GAME 1

100	75	8	3	5	9	**441**

CONUNDRUM

N	E	C	K	B	I	N	G	O

LETTER GAME 2

L	E	R	U	O	T	E	L	G

LETTER GAME 4

S	H	E	R	I	T	O	S	E

NUMBER GAME 2

25	1	7	4	2	3	**830**

SOLUTION

ROUND 79

LETTER GAME 1

C	A	N	V	O	B	I	E	C

LETTER GAME 3

F	E	N	S	T	A	B	E	A

NUMBER GAME 1

100	2	4	8	6	2	777

CONUNDRUM

M	A	R	I	E	S	W	O	E

LETTER GAME 2

T	H	O	M	A	S	T	E	Y

LETTER GAME 4

Z	E	P	I	T	M	O	I	C

NUMBER GAME 2

7	9	10	5	10	7	**842**

SOLUTION

ROUND 80

LETTER GAME 1

O	L	O	N	C	A	D	E	Y

LETTER GAME 3

P	P	H	H	O	T	A	S	E

NUMBER GAME 1

50	25	7	1	2	8	**987**

CONUNDRUM

E	A	G	L	E	T	E	D	D

LETTER GAME 2

V	I	O	N	I	A	S	N	P

LETTER GAME 4

S	L	O	T	F	E	C	K	I

NUMBER GAME 2

100	6	9	3	4	8	**678**

SOLUTION

ROUND 81

LETTER GAME 1

G	O	M	I	N	S	I	J	A

LETTER GAME 3

C	H	E	B	L	E	A	M	Z

NUMBER GAME 1

50	75	100	25	3	3	**530**

CONUNDRUM

J	O	E	L	Y	B	E	A	N

LETTER GAME 2

I	N	D	U	R	B	E	S	T

LETTER GAME 4

A	L	C	H	T	I	N	E	O

NUMBER GAME 2

100	50	25	7	5	4

333

SOLUTION

ROUND 82

LETTER GAME 1

T	T	E	E	P	P	I	S	L

LETTER GAME 3

M	O	U	N	I	S	L	E	I

NUMBER GAME 1

75	25	3	3	5	7	**659**

CONUNDRUM

U	N	I	S	O	R	T	I	N

LETTER GAME 2

S	T	H	I	R	K	C	E	A

LETTER GAME 4

A	B	S	D	P	R	E	D	E

NUMBER GAME 2

25	7	7	6	5	9	**342**

SOLUTION

ROUND 83

LETTER GAME 1

H	Y	C	A	L	L	E	B	E

LETTER GAME 3

H	U	L	F	E	S	F	D	I

NUMBER GAME 1

50	7	1	6	3	7	**827**

CONUNDRUM

N	E	A	T	P	E	T	E	R

LETTER GAME 2

F	E	L	U	D	A	T	E	D

LETTER GAME 4

C	O	G	N	A	L	I	T	S

NUMBER GAME 2

50	6	8	4	4	2	333

SOLUTION

ROUND 84

LETTER GAME 1

S	V	O	N	C	U	L	E	G

LETTER GAME 3

C	O	R	T	I	P	A	S	Y

NUMBER GAME 1

25	50	100	75	5	9	**724**

CONUNDRUM

F	I	N	E	S	T	G	I	N

LETTER GAME 2

T	H	O	S	E	P	W	A	S

LETTER GAME 4

T	A	M	I	L	E	A	E	F

NUMBER GAME 2

100	75	25	8	10	2		469

SOLUTION

ROUND 85

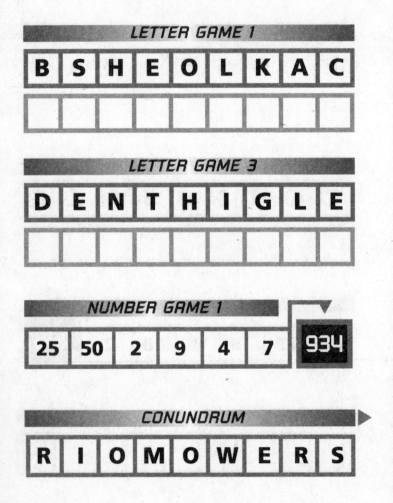

LETTER GAME 1

B	S	H	E	O	L	K	A	C

LETTER GAME 3

D	E	N	T	H	I	G	L	E

NUMBER GAME 1

| 25 | 50 | 2 | 9 | 4 | 7 |

934

CONUNDRUM

R	I	O	M	O	W	E	R	S

LETTER GAME 2

T	O	M	P	O	L	R	L	I

LETTER GAME 4

D	O	C	H	T	A	R	E	B

NUMBER GAME 2

75	9	8	2	10	1	355

SOLUTION

ROUND 86

LETTER GAME 1

W	E	B	B	O	A	T	R	P

LETTER GAME 3

C	I	N	N	O	M	G	O	D

NUMBER GAME 1

7	5	3	8	8	2	**708**

CONUNDRUM

G	I	N	G	E	R	T	U	T

LETTER GAME 2

R	I	N	T	E	L	E	J	H

LETTER GAME 4

T	E	N	B	E	A	U	N	P

NUMBER GAME 2

25	1	3	5	1	7	**444**

SOLUTION

ROUND 87

LETTER GAME 1

H	I	R	R	E	D	I	P	S

LETTER GAME 3

S	C	T	E	L	M	A	S	A

NUMBER GAME 1

100	25	2	8	10	8	**749**

CONUNDRUM

T	O	N	E	D	C	I	C	E

LETTER GAME 2

W	A	I	K	E	R	T	N	R

LETTER GAME 4

S	T	E	M	N	A	T	E	T

NUMBER GAME 2

25	3	1	6	9	8	722

SOLUTION

ROUND 88

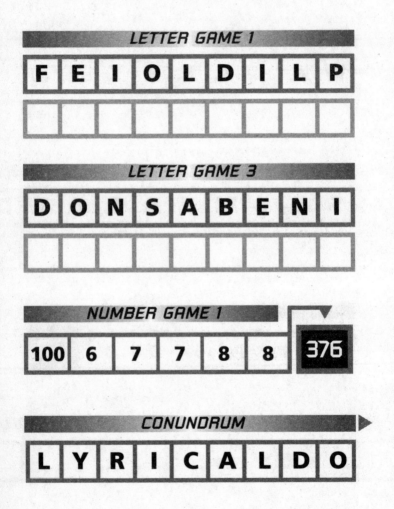

LETTER GAME 1

F	E	I	O	L	D	I	L	P

LETTER GAME 3

D	O	N	S	A	B	E	N	I

NUMBER GAME 1

100	6	7	7	8	8	**376**

CONUNDRUM

L	Y	R	I	C	A	L	D	O

LETTER GAME 2

G	R	I	B	S	A	M	R	E

LETTER GAME 4

T	H	I	S	T	E	R	I	S

NUMBER GAME 2

75	6	8	3	2	8	**993**

SOLUTION

ROUND 89

LETTER GAME 1

V	I	R	E	C	A	K	M	T

LETTER GAME 3

S	H	A	I	N	E	R	V	O

NUMBER GAME 1

75	100	8	9	7	5	**242**

CONUNDRUM

G	R	A	P	H	I	B	O	Y

LETTER GAME 2

E	X	P	I	N	C	E	L	R

LETTER GAME 4

C	L	U	N	I	P	A	B	Q

NUMBER GAME 2

25	2	3	3	1	1	**648**

SOLUTION

ROUND 90

LETTER GAME 1

S	P	U	Q	I	T	E	C	K

LETTER GAME 3

M	O	N	D	E	L	A	E	T

NUMBER GAME 1

100	50	25	7	6	1	**823**

CONUNDRUM

S	P	E	R	S	I	L	A	D

LETTER GAME 2

H	O	S	R	M	A	C	K	E

LETTER GAME 4

S	H	O	R	P	Y	A	D	I

NUMBER GAME 2

9	3	10	10	7	5	**854**

SOLUTION

ROUND 91

LETTER GAME 1

S	U	S	O	D	E	L	R	O

LETTER GAME 3

C	H	P	O	R	I	U	E	G

NUMBER GAME 1

100	75	50	25	7	7	**918**

CONUNDRUM

O	C	E	A	N	W	A	L	L

LETTER GAME 2

S	O	L	I	N	F	E	E	T

LETTER GAME 4

S	T	E	R	A	T	O	P	M

NUMBER GAME 2

100	50	6	4	1	5		783

SOLUTION

ROUND 92

LETTER GAME 1

W	R	I	D	E	B	L	E	T

LETTER GAME 3

L	U	R	I	C	A	S	T	O

NUMBER GAME 1

75	9	9	1	2	1	**732**

CONUNDRUM

C	R	I	M	A	T	I	O	N

LETTER GAME 2

L	W	E	G	I	N	C	A	R

LETTER GAME 4

C	L	O	M	I	B	S	H	A

NUMBER GAME 2

25	3	4	8	10	10		615

SOLUTION

ROUND 93

LETTER GAME 1

T	H	O	O	B	S	E	A	U

LETTER GAME 3

B	I	W	S	I	N	G	N	E

NUMBER GAME 1

100	75	50	10	9	8

944

CONUNDRUM

N	I	C	K	E	R	B	I	G

LETTER GAME 2

C	R	E	T	I	G	A	N	R

LETTER GAME 4

U	N	D	E	N	O	C	E	X

NUMBER GAME 2

75	25	4	8	9	7	**978**

SOLUTION

ROUND 94

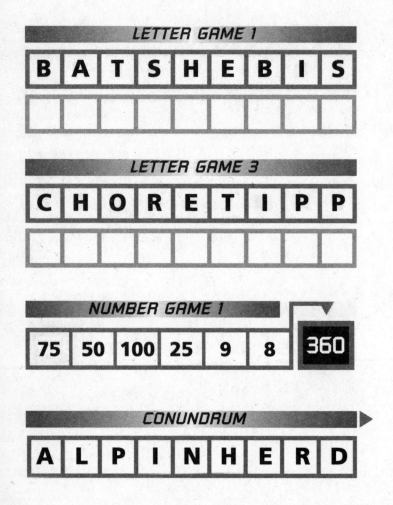

LETTER GAME 1

| B | A | T | S | H | E | B | I | S |

LETTER GAME 3

| C | H | O | R | E | T | I | P | P |

NUMBER GAME 1

| 75 | 50 | 100 | 25 | 9 | 8 | **360** |

CONUNDRUM

| A | L | P | I | N | H | E | R | D |

LETTER GAME 2

A	G	I	L	L	P	E	X	S

LETTER GAME 4

E	M	M	L	I	S	T	A	C

NUMBER GAME 2

6	7	10	8	3	8	**592**

SOLUTION

ROUND 95

LETTER GAME 1

F	O	O	R	G	I	N	P	W

LETTER GAME 3

S	T	U	R	N	I	M	E	O

NUMBER GAME 1

25	9	7	2	10	1	585

CONUNDRUM

C	L	I	F	F	D	U	T	I

LETTER GAME 2

S	A	R	B	E	I	S	R	E

LETTER GAME 4

H	U	B	C	L	O	U	S	E

NUMBER GAME 2

100	3	6	2	2	1		**555**

SOLUTION

ROUND 96

LETTER GAME 1

A	N	R	A	T	T	E	R	D

LETTER GAME 3

T	R	O	M	A	E	G	E	S

NUMBER GAME 1

75	50	25	5	4	4	**637**

CONUNDRUM

R	A	P	R	A	P	H	A	G

LETTER GAME 2

A	L	M	E	N	T	I	U	C

LETTER GAME 4

Y	I	N	T	O	R	S	I	E

NUMBER GAME 2

50	75	4	4	8	2	547

SOLUTION

ROUND 97

LETTER GAME 1

N	U	M	T	I	C	P	A	E

LETTER GAME 3

G	U	R	N	D	A	H	E	A

NUMBER GAME 1

50	6	5	7	9	4	**679**

CONUNDRUM

N	O	S	E	S	H	R	U	G

LETTER GAME 2

N	N	H	O	P	R	L	A	E

LETTER GAME 4

T	H	E	I	R	G	A	W	N

NUMBER GAME 2

100	7	5	3	9	6		237

SOLUTION

ROUND 98

LETTER GAME 1

A	R	C	U	S	T	E	A	C

LETTER GAME 3

Y	A	C	I	L	L	B	N	U

NUMBER GAME 1

6	3	8	8	3	7	**941**

CONUNDRUM

S	O	N	I	C	L	U	N	I

LETTER GAME 2

M	U	T	I	Q	E	E	S	U

LETTER GAME 4

E	E	N	B	I	R	G	D	A

NUMBER GAME 2

50	8	7	2	1	4	689

SOLUTION

ROUND 99

LETTER GAME 1

D	I	J	A	N	C	E	U	R

LETTER GAME 3

C	E	T	O	L	L	A	D	A

NUMBER GAME 1

50	75	5	3	4	4	**726**

CONUNDRUM

N	I	C	K	S	Q	U	A	D

LETTER GAME 2

A	R	T	E	N	G	E	E	H

LETTER GAME 4

Q	U	E	B	I	Z	E	T	P

NUMBER GAME 2

75	4	6	6	5	3	**849**

SOLUTION

ROUND 100

F	I	L	D	O	M	A	N	D

D	E	T	E	N	C	I	C	O

NUMBER GAME 1

75	50	25	8	2	3	**927**

CONUNDRUM

B	U	N	D	U	T	O	E	D

LETTER GAME 2

G	U	S	T	I	P	E	D	O

LETTER GAME 4

A	A	B	G	E	L	I	R	C

NUMBER GAME 2

50	100	25	75	4	4	**693**

SOLUTION

ROUND 101

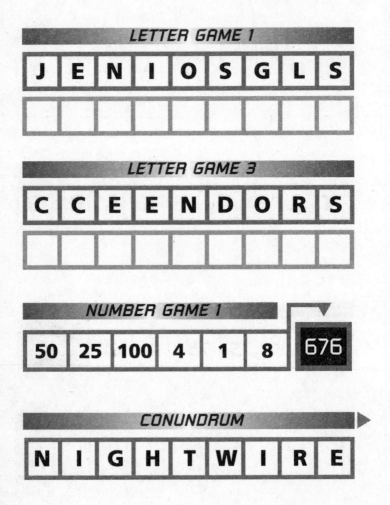

LETTER GAME 1

J	E	N	I	O	S	G	L	S

LETTER GAME 3

C	C	E	E	N	D	O	R	S

NUMBER GAME 1

| 50 | 25 | 100 | 4 | 1 | 8 |

676

CONUNDRUM

N	I	G	H	T	W	I	R	E

LETTER GAME 2

G	R	V	I	N	Y	C	E	A

LETTER GAME 4

T	L	P	A	E	O	Y	N	R

NUMBER GAME 2

100	6	5	7	6	4	**849**

SOLUTION

ROUND 102

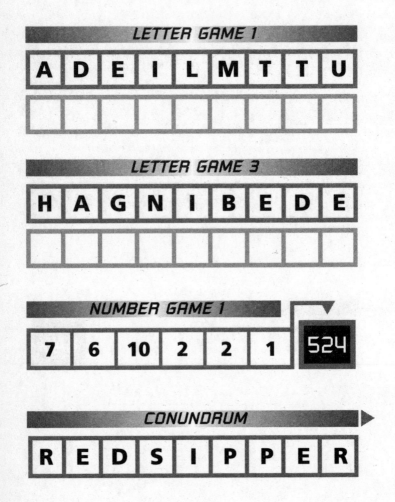

LETTER GAME 1

A	D	E	I	L	M	T	T	U

LETTER GAME 3

H	A	G	N	I	B	E	D	E

NUMBER GAME 1

7	6	10	2	2	1	**524**

CONUNDRUM

R	E	D	S	I	P	P	E	R

LETTER GAME 2

O	O	T	H	P	A	S	T	E

LETTER GAME 4

E	H	I	O	P	S	U	R	V

NUMBER GAME 2

50	7	2	8	9	1	875

SOLUTION

ROUND 103

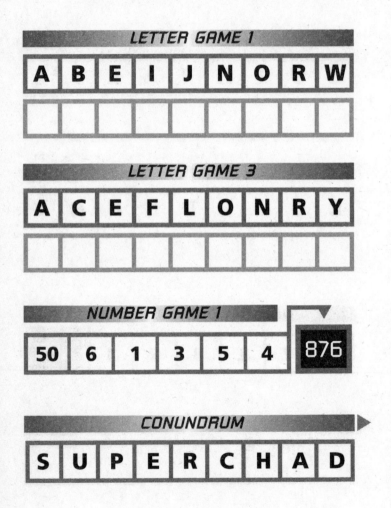

LETTER GAME 1

| A | B | E | I | J | N | O | R | W |

LETTER GAME 3

| A | C | E | F | L | O | N | R | Y |

NUMBER GAME 1

| 50 | 6 | 1 | 3 | 5 | 4 | | 876 |

CONUNDRUM

| S | U | P | E | R | C | H | A | D |

LETTER GAME 2

N	T	Z	O	A	I	P	R	E

LETTER GAME 4

B	O	J	E	D	G	A	N	A

NUMBER GAME 2

75	7	5	1	1	3	**666**

SOLUTION

ROUND 104

LETTER GAME 1

X	A	T	G	A	L	H	E	W

LETTER GAME 3

O	I	S	N	V	A	D	E	H

NUMBER GAME 1

50	7	3	6	9	5	988

CONUNDRUM

N	E	V	E	R	W	I	T	I

LETTER GAME 2

L	R	M	E	O	T	N	I	V

LETTER GAME 4

T	A	N	O	V	U	G	T	E

NUMBER GAME 2

4	9	8	8	2	1	650

SOLUTION

ROUND 105

LETTER GAME 1

P	O	R	A	C	E	T	O	V

LETTER GAME 3

Z	D	P	I	O	M	T	E	H

NUMBER GAME 1

25	3	7	10	5	6		624

CONUNDRUM

M	A	L	E	T	U	N	I	C

LETTER GAME 2

R	A	I	R	E	B	L	Y	Z

LETTER GAME 4

U	P	T	H	E	N	O	S	E

NUMBER GAME 2

100	75	3	3	4	6	**849**

SOLUTION

ROUND 106

LETTER GAME 1

A	E	M	P	R	O	S	T	U

LETTER GAME 3

T	E	I	N	D	L	Q	U	O

NUMBER GAME 1

100	8	1	7	9	5	**329**

CONUNDRUM

L	A	B	N	U	T	T	E	R

LETTER GAME 2

N	D	E	A	M	L	I	C	E

LETTER GAME 4

D	T	I	N	O	M	A	N	E

NUMBER GAME 2

25	7	4	1	7	4	**465**

SOLUTION

ROUND 107

LETTER GAME 1

S	U	E	T	Y	O	I	S	L

LETTER GAME 3

Q	I	U	A	E	R	F	G	H

NUMBER GAME 1

50	8	7	5	3	2	**916**

CONUNDRUM

T	A	R	T	I	R	U	B	Y

LETTER GAME 2

B	G	F	A	O	I	E	R	T

LETTER GAME 4

S	P	O	I	G	M	E	O	B

NUMBER GAME 2

75	4	3	5	4	1	860

SOLUTION

ROUND 108

LETTER GAME 1

L	X	P	E	A	E	F	H	M

LETTER GAME 3

R	C	T	M	A	I	E	G	D

NUMBER GAME 1

25	9	10	8	2	2	**781**

CONUNDRUM

M	I	N	E	R	B	U	N	G

LETTER GAME 2

L	R	G	O	E	O	S	N	C

LETTER GAME 4

S	N	W	O	I	A	T	P	U

NUMBER GAME 2

25	4	3	3	1	2	923

SOLUTION

ROUND 109

LETTER GAME 1

R	D	G	O	E	V	A	R	P

LETTER GAME 3

D	M	S	M	E	I	A	S	L

NUMBER GAME 1

100	6	8	4	1	1	526

CONUNDRUM

G	I	A	N	T	B	E	R	T

LETTER GAME 2

N	O	D	I	F	A	E	T	S

LETTER GAME 4

A	S	C	E	D	A	C	H	D

NUMBER GAME 2

75	8	5	2	9	2	**864**

SOLUTION

ROUND 110

LETTER GAME 1

G	U	T	T	A	P	O	E	R

LETTER GAME 3

I	M	U	V	N	E	C	A	R

NUMBER GAME 1

10	2	6	7	5	1	842

CONUNDRUM

P	A	S	T	E	I	G	H	T

LETTER GAME 2

N	I	S	D	A	N	V	E	H

LETTER GAME 4

A	T	H	E	R	T	O	N	S

NUMBER GAME 2

9	6	3	8	2	9	**586**

SOLUTION

ROUND 111

LETTER GAME 1

M	A	T	Y	V	O	L	N	E

LETTER GAME 3

A	T	G	R	A	E	K	X	U

NUMBER GAME 1

75	4	6	8	5	5		795

CONUNDRUM

I	C	E	S	I	N	N	E	R

LETTER GAME 2

N	E	S	O	L	C	G	E	Z

LETTER GAME 4

W	O	I	T	H	R	S	E	E

NUMBER GAME 2

100	10	9	8	2	7	468

SOLUTION

ROUND 112

N	H	T	E	I	J	R	E	A

LETTER GAME 3

C	L	O	E	T	D	I	P	E

NUMBER GAME 1

50	25	6	6	4	4	**820**

CONUNDRUM

S	I	N	N	E	R	D	O	G

LETTER GAME 2

O	L	C	X	S	E	A	O	V

LETTER GAME 4

M	T	C	N	I	E	O	A	I

NUMBER GAME 2

25	2	5	6	5	3	**311**

SOLUTION

ROUND 113

LETTER GAME 1

D	T	E	I	P	S	E	N	O

LETTER GAME 3

W	T	M	E	A	I	R	D	S

NUMBER GAME 1

100	7	6	3	2	10	805

CONUNDRUM

N	I	C	E	Q	U	E	S	T

LETTER GAME 2

C	X	O	A	L	U	R	N	O

LETTER GAME 4

C	S	E	O	T	H	E	M	F

NUMBER GAME 2

50	3	9	3	9	6	729

SOLUTION

ROUND 114

LETTER GAME 1

D	N	P	U	E	I	K	T	L

LETTER GAME 3

D	P	E	O	H	S	E	G	O

NUMBER GAME 1

100	10	10	9	9	1	**629**

CONUNDRUM

S	E	M	I	S	T	I	L	L

LETTER GAME 2

F	C	L	D	I	O	E	V	R

LETTER GAME 4

H	R	B	A	T	I	A	T	E

NUMBER GAME 2

25	50	75	100	9	6	840

SOLUTION

ROUND 115

LETTER GAME 1

L	T	N	G	E	U	O	D	L

LETTER GAME 3

P	S	I	O	T	G	A	P	H

NUMBER GAME 1

25	1	4	1	3	8	622

CONUNDRUM

I	N	T	R	O	A	I	D	A

LETTER GAME 2

C	R	H	R	W	E	A	O	M

LETTER GAME 4

N	I	G	Y	E	S	A	V	S

NUMBER GAME 2

50	100	75	3	4	4		659

SOLUTION

ROUND 116

LETTER GAME 1

B	H	E	I	D	O	T	U	R

LETTER GAME 3

P	R	N	D	E	A	S	O	C

NUMBER GAME 1

75	6	2	4	4	8	555

CONUNDRUM

E	N	O	U	G	H	D	E	T

LETTER GAME 2

A	O	P	L	I	Y	E	L	G

LETTER GAME 4

T	G	Y	I	E	D	S	W	A

NUMBER GAME 2

2	8	7	7	5	1	**343**

SOLUTION

ROUND 117

LETTER GAME 1

G X A H E T P N O

LETTER GAME 3

E N Q T U O L P E

NUMBER GAME 1

| 100 | 1 | 7 | 9 | 6 | 5 | 248 |

CONUNDRUM

L I T T L E S E A

LETTER GAME 2

E	F	G	I	N	O	R	V	T

LETTER GAME 4

A	D	E	I	L	M	N	S	T

NUMBER GAME 2

10	2	10	5	4	6	740

SOLUTION

ROUND 118

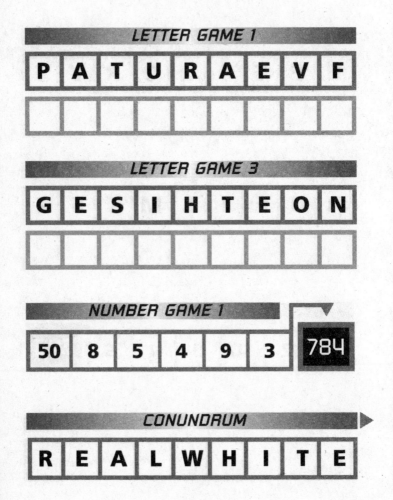

LETTER GAME 1

P	A	T	U	R	A	E	V	F

LETTER GAME 3

G	E	S	I	H	T	E	O	N

NUMBER GAME 1

50	8	5	4	9	3	**784**

CONUNDRUM

R	E	A	L	W	H	I	T	E

LETTER GAME 2

N	E	T	U	S	T	A	F	E

LETTER GAME 4

N	U	R	I	S	M	I	V	E

NUMBER GAME 2

50	25	7	2	8	4		693

SOLUTION

ROUND 119

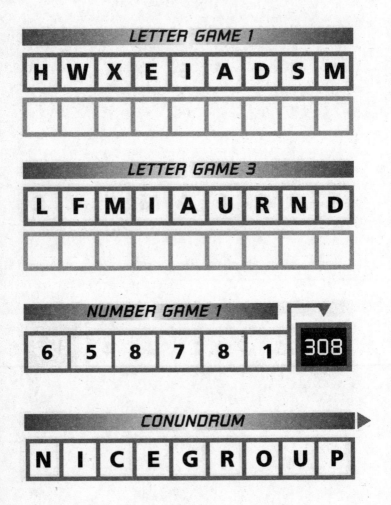

LETTER GAME 1

H	W	X	E	I	A	D	S	M

LETTER GAME 3

L	F	M	I	A	U	R	N	D

NUMBER GAME 1

6	5	8	7	8	1	308

CONUNDRUM

N	I	C	E	G	R	O	U	P

LETTER GAME 2

L	M	W	O	E	O	E	N	T

LETTER GAME 4

L	R	E	E	A	G	S	C	L

NUMBER GAME 2

25	2	4	3	3	5	**837**

SOLUTION

ROUND 120

U	C	E	D	P	I	G	N	N

A	S	C	O	O	G	R	E	L

50	6	3	7	7	4	**264**

D	A	R	N	S	C	E	N	T

LETTER GAME 2

T	O	R	I	E	I	F	V	L

LETTER GAME 4

R	M	D	E	I	T	S	A	U

NUMBER GAME 2

9	7	4	2	1	6	**750**

SOLUTION

ROUND 121

LETTER GAME 2

S	R	T	M	F	O	A	O	K

LETTER GAME 4

U	A	E	N	C	L	P	O	S

NUMBER GAME 2

75	50	100	8	3	1	**264**

SOLUTION

ROUND 122

LETTER GAME 1

T	R	F	O	E	I	L	Y	R

LETTER GAME 3

O	H	E	X	I	D	A	P	E

NUMBER GAME 1

6	2	9	5	2	1	580

CONUNDRUM

S	A	T	A	N	L	I	T	E

LETTER GAME 2

R	H	Y	S	E	A	O	C	B

LETTER GAME 4

G	R	P	Y	O	U	E	N	G

NUMBER GAME 2

25	5	2	3	2	8	**777**

SOLUTION

ROUND 123

LETTER GAME 1

M	L	T	I	E	O	J	R	S

LETTER GAME 3

F	T	S	T	I	E	U	A	M

NUMBER GAME 1

| 50 | 9 | 6 | 4 | 10 | 6 |

914

CONUNDRUM

O	G	R	E	Q	U	E	S	T

LETTER GAME 2

B	N	A	C	O	T	G	E	S

LETTER GAME 4

A	V	E	N	R	I	U	G	A

NUMBER GAME 2

100	50	25	3	8	7	819

SOLUTION

ROUND 124

LETTER GAME 1

P	F	A	E	R	D	I	M	E

LETTER GAME 3

S	C	S	T	O	E	I	R	X

NUMBER GAME 1

75	9	10	9	10	5	**444**

CONUNDRUM

S	P	E	E	D	B	A	R	D

LETTER GAME 2

M	T	S	H	O	O	R	A	D

LETTER GAME 4

G	I	C	A	E	T	K	O	D

NUMBER GAME 2

25	1	6	7	8	8	**533**

SOLUTION

ROUND 125

LETTER GAME 1

T	Z	E	N	I	G	N	A	E

LETTER GAME 3

Y	D	F	A	I	L	R	A	T

NUMBER GAME 1

25	100	7	4	2	3	620

CONUNDRUM

A	S	K	F	O	R	G	I	N

LETTER GAME 2

R	P	W	O	E	T	S	O	E

LETTER GAME 4

L	Y	P	R	U	E	E	I	Q

NUMBER GAME 2

75	8	8	6	7	7	**931**

SOLUTION

ROUND 126

LETTER GAME 1

R	L	D	O	E	A	V	M	N

LETTER GAME 3

G	D	B	S	E	T	O	C	E

NUMBER GAME 1

50	3	2	10	4	8	**642**

CONUNDRUM

T	R	I	C	O	R	N	E	C

LETTER GAME 2

P	R	N	I	E	R	S	I	F

LETTER GAME 4

G	E	T	N	G	O	R	A	B

NUMBER GAME 2

4	7	8	9	5	2	**253**

SOLUTION

ROUND 127

LETTER GAME 1

T	D	J	E	I	U	R	T	E

LETTER GAME 3

M	S	P	F	I	A	E	L	H

NUMBER GAME 1

100	75	6	2	5	1	464

CONUNDRUM

I	L	O	V	E	U	N	O	T

LETTER GAME 2

E	O	T	R	I	A	N	D	P

LETTER GAME 4

O	F	S	R	E	C	G	U	T

NUMBER GAME 2

8	10	4	3	1	7	875

SOLUTION

ROUND 128

LETTER GAME 1

H	U	G	L	A	N	S	E	I

LETTER GAME 3

A	V	E	N	D	U	G	R	E

NUMBER GAME 1

25	75	100	6	9	6	**386**

CONUNDRUM

C	R	U	E	L	B	A	I	T

LETTER GAME 2

O	S	L	D	E	N	W	L	A

LETTER GAME 4

G	O	Y	R	E	H	U	D	N

NUMBER GAME 2

75	6	3	8	8	3	697

SOLUTION

ROUND 129

LETTER GAME 1

O	E	I	D	N	R	A	R	N

LETTER GAME 3

R	C	C	E	U	E	T	M	L

NUMBER GAME 1

100	2	5	5	6	7	868

CONUNDRUM

G	U	E	S	T	P	I	N	T

LETTER GAME 2

S	M	R	N	I	E	U	A	R

LETTER GAME 4

L	T	O	A	N	D	C	B	E

NUMBER GAME 2

50	8	7	4	9	1	274

SOLUTION

ROUND 130

LETTER GAME 1

T	N	D	E	A	E	L	C	O

LETTER GAME 3

E	I	A	N	R	K	Z	S	N

NUMBER GAME 1

25	4	10	5	7	3	523

CONUNDRUM

S	E	C	U	R	E	P	O	T

LETTER GAME 2

G	U	R	E	S	I	L	O	G

LETTER GAME 4

X	U	J	O	I	B	K	E	D

NUMBER GAME 2

25	2	9	10	9	7	**821**

SOLUTION

ROUND 131

LETTER GAME 1

T	A	G	L	A	V	E	O	C

LETTER GAME 3

P	I	N	D	U	S	O	R	E

NUMBER GAME 1

50	4	4	2	3	6	**377**

CONUNDRUM

C	O	C	O	A	R	I	N	D

LETTER GAME 2

T	D	N	I	U	I	M	L	O

LETTER GAME 4

S	P	V	E	U	A	T	Z	S

NUMBER GAME 2

75	8	3	6	6	7	**948**

SOLUTION

ROUND 132

LETTER GAME 1

V	A	T	P	E	C	A	L	O

LETTER GAME 3

D	S	E	O	G	X	N	E	P

NUMBER GAME 1

25	50	75	100	3	3

741

CONUNDRUM

F	I	G	F	R	I	E	N	D

LETTER GAME 2

E	I	J	N	O	S	S	T	T

LETTER GAME 4

A	C	E	I	I	M	R	S	T

NUMBER GAME 2

5	2	7	9	7	9	**144**

SOLUTION

ROUND 133

LETTER GAME 1

Y	D	G	I	E	I	R	N	O

LETTER GAME 3

U	E	A	R	D	W	V	L	O

NUMBER GAME 1

25	3	10	4	5	7	937

CONUNDRUM

D	U	N	D	E	E	P	O	X

LETTER GAME 2

A	D	D	E	G	I	N	O	S

LETTER GAME 4

D	D	U	U	N	R	S	E	E

NUMBER GAME 2

100	6	9	9	2	2	826

SOLUTION

ROUND 134

LETTER GAME 1

L	W	O	D	S	L	I	O	E

LETTER GAME 3

E	I	G	Y	U	D	R	H	S

NUMBER GAME 1

25	2	8	7	7	5	**914**

CONUNDRUM

T	O	U	G	H	P	A	R	A

LETTER GAME 2

A	L	U	T	O	A	V	E	N

LETTER GAME 4

N	A	R	O	F	Y	L	E	P

NUMBER GAME 2

50	25	75	3	6	8	623

SOLUTION

ROUND 135

LETTER GAME 1

L	E	P	S	E	Z	R	I	Y

LETTER GAME 3

P	E	L	I	M	T	U	R	C

NUMBER GAME 1

75	100	2	4	9	7	**578**

CONUNDRUM

D	E	P	T	S	T	O	R	E

LETTER GAME 2

N	O	S	I	H	O	A	R	U

LETTER GAME 4

D	C	U	E	W	S	O	I	D

NUMBER GAME 2

50	8	1	7	6	1	239

SOLUTION

ROUND 136

LETTER GAME 1

O	G	H	A	I	T	L	R	S

LETTER GAME 3

D	R	A	I	W	I	G	N	P

NUMBER GAME 1

100	10	5	6	9	2	471

CONUNDRUM

S	A	U	C	E	T	O	F	F

LETTER GAME 2

G	R	T	A	D	I	S	E	S

LETTER GAME 4

C	E	L	E	D	A	T	A	S

NUMBER GAME 2

75	25	100	50	2	2	704

SOLUTION

ROUND 137

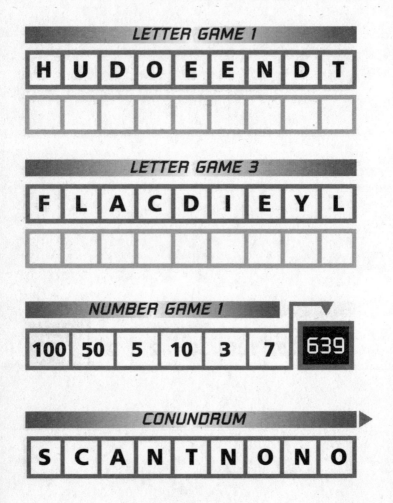

LETTER GAME 1

H	U	D	O	E	E	N	D	T

LETTER GAME 3

F	L	A	C	D	I	E	Y	L

NUMBER GAME 1

100	50	5	10	3	7	639

CONUNDRUM

S	C	A	N	T	N	O	N	O

LETTER GAME 2

S	F	R	L	H	O	U	I	E

LETTER GAME 4

T	R	T	I	E	I	D	V	D

NUMBER GAME 2

6	7	4	4	3	1	**294**

SOLUTION

ROUND 138

LETTER GAME 1

A	Y	D	E	I	O	V	P	L

LETTER GAME 3

Y	H	M	T	P	U	I	D	E

NUMBER GAME 1

25	10	2	4	7	2	555

CONUNDRUM

I	M	N	O	G	H	O	S	T

LETTER GAME 2

O	E	I	T	F	S	X	A	D

LETTER GAME 4

G	D	C	I	A	E	O	T	B

NUMBER GAME 2

10	3	2	8	9	1	584

SOLUTION

ROUND 139

LETTER GAME 1

L	G	A	I	P	S	A	R	B

LETTER GAME 3

L	R	Z	O	A	E	R	M	T

NUMBER GAME 1

75	8	10	9	8	9	244

CONUNDRUM

E	D	D	Y	H	A	R	T	E

LETTER GAME 2

A	S	K	R	O	L	Y	C	I

LETTER GAME 4

L	R	Z	L	U	E	I	G	Y

NUMBER GAME 2

50	75	2	3	1	9	**186**

SOLUTION

ROUND 140

LETTER GAME 1

B	E	I	O	R	S	T	U	V

LETTER GAME 3

O	C	A	T	G	E	H	P	D

NUMBER GAME 1

25	4	1	10	10	1	875

CONUNDRUM

G	O	L	D	E	N	A	C	E

LETTER GAME 2

B	S	U	X	R	E	L	H	A

LETTER GAME 4

A	A	C	D	E	I	L	L	N

NUMBER GAME 2

50	7	10	8	8	5	933

SOLUTION

ROUND 141

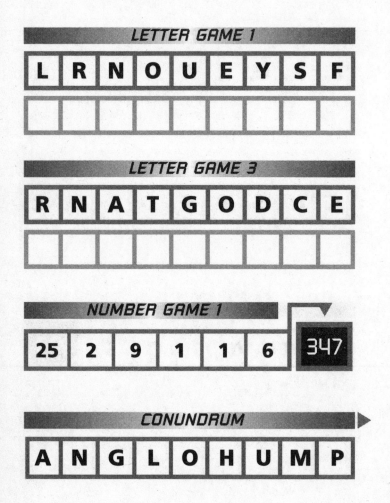

LETTER GAME 1

L	R	N	O	U	E	Y	S	F

LETTER GAME 3

R	N	A	T	G	O	D	C	E

NUMBER GAME 1

25	2	9	1	1	6	**347**

CONUNDRUM

A	N	G	L	O	H	U	M	P

LETTER GAME 2

C	R	E	I	D	O	L	V	Y

LETTER GAME 4

C	M	S	A	E	O	G	U	L

NUMBER GAME 2

50	100	8	7	9	10		311

SOLUTION

ROUND 142

LETTER GAME 1

O	S	T	E	Y	R	A	B	U

LETTER GAME 3

S	B	I	A	S	T	O	U	S

NUMBER GAME 1

25	10	7	4	4	2	**812**

CONUNDRUM

T	H	I	S	G	N	O	M	E

LETTER GAME 2

N	L	R	E	U	S	G	W	A

LETTER GAME 4

B	O	P	D	A	N	G	I	R

NUMBER GAME 2

75	25	50	100	4	9	**606**

SOLUTION

ROUND 143

LETTER GAME 1

E	N	V	U	I	J	S	K	R

LETTER GAME 3

E	O	E	B	N	T	Y	A	G

NUMBER GAME 1

50	6	10	2	9	7	871

CONUNDRUM

D	A	D	S	B	O	N	C	E

LETTER GAME 2

G	Z	N	U	E	A	S	L	D

LETTER GAME 4

A	L	B	O	T	E	R	E	I

NUMBER GAME 2

100	6	7	2	2	5	372

SOLUTION

ROUND 144

LETTER GAME 1

N	G	H	E	I	E	D	T	N

LETTER GAME 3

T	S	V	N	O	I	U	D	A

NUMBER GAME 1

4	5	2	3	1	6	840

CONUNDRUM

T	I	N	Y	T	A	M	E	R

LETTER GAME 2

T	I	M	L	O	P	E	D	S

LETTER GAME 4

L	K	T	A	E	P	R	A	C

NUMBER GAME 2

8	3	4	1	2	3	**864**

SOLUTION

ROUND 145

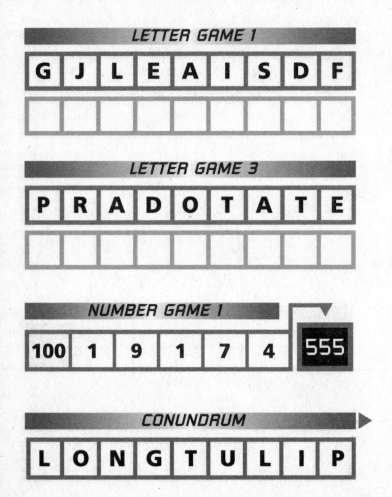

LETTER GAME 1

G	J	L	E	A	I	S	D	F

LETTER GAME 3

P	R	A	D	O	T	A	T	E

NUMBER GAME 1

100	1	9	1	7	4	555

CONUNDRUM

L	O	N	G	T	U	L	I	P

LETTER GAME 2

S	A	R	T	O	E	S	K	B

LETTER GAME 4

N	B	N	E	A	I	L	P	S

NUMBER GAME 2

10	9	10	8	7	7	226

SOLUTION

ROUND 146

LETTER GAME 1

T	L	R	I	E	G	M	A	R

LETTER GAME 3

H	I	N	S	A	G	L	O	T

NUMBER GAME 1

25	7	5	4	1	10	628

CONUNDRUM

T	Y	P	I	C	A	L	E	S

LETTER GAME 2

C	S	I	N	A	R	P	E	N

LETTER GAME 4

M	A	R	T	Y	O	R	N	E

NUMBER GAME 2

50	6	8	2	1	3	**867**

SOLUTION

ROUND 147

LETTER GAME 1

G	I	F	A	T	O	U	E	R

LETTER GAME 3

G	H	S	I	U	O	L	F	K

NUMBER GAME 1

75	25	8	3	9	7	**945**

CONUNDRUM

T	R	I	A	D	R	I	T	E

LETTER GAME 2

Y	A	C	D	G	T	E	R	O

LETTER GAME 4

A	C	E	E	I	F	N	R	T

NUMBER GAME 2

100	75	50	4	10	5	885

SOLUTION

ROUND 148

LETTER GAME 1

N	D	E	A	M	L	I	W	R

LETTER GAME 3

N	O	I	N	I	T	F	G	Y

NUMBER GAME 1

25	50	7	9	2	3	944

CONUNDRUM

F	O	R	D	C	O	M	E	T

LETTER GAME 2

E	A	S	S	M	I	T	R	F

LETTER GAME 4

I	E	R	F	B	T	O	S	E

NUMBER GAME 2

50	6	8	8	1	7	867

SOLUTION

ROUND 149

LETTER GAME 1

A	V	T	I	R	E	D	L	U

LETTER GAME 3

S	N	E	A	G	L	M	I	G

NUMBER GAME 1

75	5	9	7	4	3	**573**

CONUNDRUM

D	I	R	T	Y	R	O	O	M

LETTER GAME 2

F	G	R	O	I	E	S	H	L

LETTER GAME 4

Y	V	U	S	D	I	E	N	T

NUMBER GAME 2

25	50	100	6	6	9		693

SOLUTION

ROUND 150

U	P	N	T	I	A	K	D	O

Z	I	U	E	N	X	A	S	D

50	4	10	5	10	3	**987**

T	E	L	Y	A	N	G	E	L

LETTER GAME 2

L	I	M	A	H	I	G	S	R

LETTER GAME 4

K	S	U	P	G	A	O	D	E

NUMBER GAME 2

75	2	2	3	8	5	704

SOLUTION

ROUND 151

LETTER GAME 1

B	I	M	O	N	A	L	M	A

LETTER GAME 3

L	E	G	A	S	N	Y	I	C

NUMBER GAME 1

100	10	1	8	3	8	716

CONUNDRUM

P	R	E	P	A	G	A	I	N

LETTER GAME 2

T	S	O	E	A	C	J	N	I

LETTER GAME 4

K	A	T	J	E	A	T	D	N

NUMBER GAME 2

25	2	3	1	10	9	**462**

SOLUTION

ROUND 152

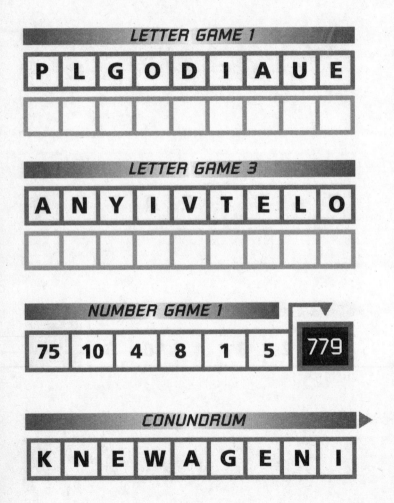

LETTER GAME 1

P	L	G	O	D	I	A	U	E

LETTER GAME 3

A	N	Y	I	V	T	E	L	O

NUMBER GAME 1

75	10	4	8	1	5	779

CONUNDRUM

K	N	E	W	A	G	E	N	I

LETTER GAME 2

E	H	E	I	L	D	A	N	W

LETTER GAME 4

R	O	N	E	T	J	U	I	P

NUMBER GAME 2

7	2	8	5	6	2	**904**

SOLUTION

ROUND 153

LETTER GAME 1

J	N	S	U	A	C	E	N	T

LETTER GAME 3

G	R	I	E	A	N	W	N	E

NUMBER GAME 1

100	2	9	7	10	10	404

CONUNDRUM

D	U	D	R	E	P	O	R	T

LETTER GAME 2

N	G	T	E	A	O	B	I	J

LETTER GAME 4

R	D	G	E	A	E	T	V	T

NUMBER GAME 2

50	5	1	3	4	1	686

SOLUTION

ROUND 154

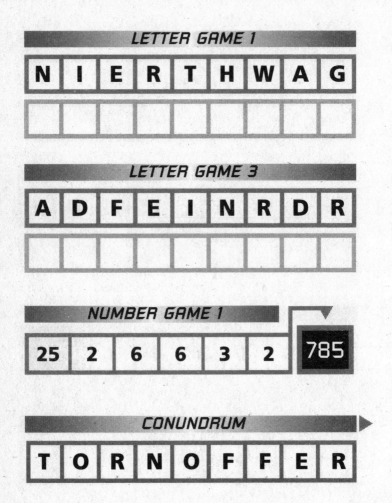

LETTER GAME 1

N	I	E	R	T	H	W	A	G

LETTER GAME 3

A	D	F	E	I	N	R	D	R

NUMBER GAME 1

25	2	6	6	3	2	785

CONUNDRUM

T	O	R	N	O	F	F	E	R

LETTER GAME 2

Y	B	G	F	A	A	U	E	R

LETTER GAME 4

S	M	T	E	S	P	U	D	I

NUMBER GAME 2

75	6	2	2	1	1	**290**

SOLUTION

ROUND 155

LETTER GAME 1

B	T	A	A	C	L	E	H	E

LETTER GAME 3

E	L	T	D	T	E	E	R	A

NUMBER GAME 1

50	7	8	9	10	10	**356**

CONUNDRUM

G	I	V	E	R	O	U	N	D

LETTER GAME 2

O	S	C	H	A	Z	E	P	Y

LETTER GAME 4

G	M	R	A	E	N	C	O	H

NUMBER GAME 2

8	5	2	1	9	9	**748**

SOLUTION

ROUND 156

S	U	O	L	V	I	C	E	S

LETTER GAME 3

G	O	R	V	I	T	A	N	D

NUMBER GAME 1

75	5	7	3	1	9	**642**

CONUNDRUM

M	A	N	I	C	A	B	L	E

LETTER GAME 2

D	O	S	R	I	W	O	N	D

LETTER GAME 4

F	A	L	R	Y	U	P	E	I

NUMBER GAME 2

100	4	4	2	1	3		960

SOLUTION

ROUND 157

C	O	B	R	E	L	O	E	H

F	A	D	E	G	T	O	P	O

NUMBER GAME 1

50	25	75	8	3	6		299

CONUNDRUM

C	U	T	E	F	A	U	L	T

LETTER GAME 2

C	P	B	R	Y	E	I	E	R

LETTER GAME 4

R	M	D	A	O	T	V	E	A

NUMBER GAME 2

25	4	1	9	6	2	**333**

SOLUTION

ROUND 158

LETTER GAME 1

G	R	O	W	I	L	M	A	N

LETTER GAME 3

A	C	H	I	D	N	E	T	S

NUMBER GAME 1

10	6	7	5	5	3	**963**

CONUNDRUM

T	E	A	T	U	L	I	P	S

LETTER GAME 2

A	P	D	L	U	A	R	G	E

LETTER GAME 4

R	S	B	I	O	T	D	E	O

NUMBER GAME 2

100	8	2	3	7	4	**966**

SOLUTION

ROUND 159

LETTER GAME 1

A	D	A	C	W	K	R	B	E

LETTER GAME 3

D	C	R	A	S	P	I	E	P

NUMBER GAME 1

75	1	2	3	4	5	704

CONUNDRUM

C	A	N	D	I	D	O	T	I

LETTER GAME 2

L	L	W	O	E	S	I	R	T

LETTER GAME 4

F	T	W	E	O	E	S	L	N

NUMBER GAME 2

25	8	4	3	3	6	527

SOLUTION

ROUND 160

LETTER GAME 1

S	U	E	Q	Y	B	R	A	L

LETTER GAME 3

E	D	H	L	E	A	T	F	I

NUMBER GAME 1

25	7	1	6	9	2	478

CONUNDRUM

C	L	E	A	N	C	O	D	E

336

LETTER GAME 2

D	Y	L	H	I	T	S	O	A

LETTER GAME 4

O	F	S	G	I	X	D	E	H

NUMBER GAME 2

25	6	3	9	2	4	**938**

SOLUTION

ROUND 161

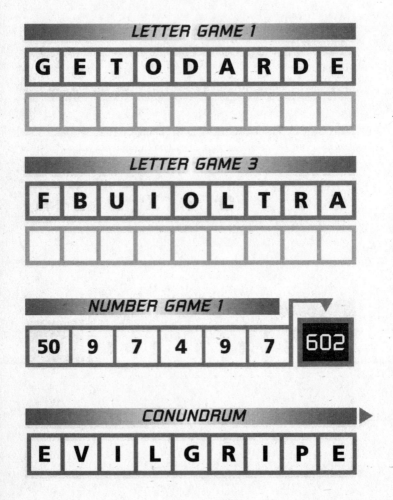

LETTER GAME 1

G	E	T	O	D	A	R	D	E

LETTER GAME 3

F	B	U	I	O	L	T	R	A

NUMBER GAME 1

50	9	7	4	9	7	**602**

CONUNDRUM

E	V	I	L	G	R	I	P	E

LETTER GAME 2

R	T	O	P	C	B	L	A	I

LETTER GAME 4

T	Y	P	O	S	T	R	E	A

NUMBER GAME 2

100	5	10	4	6	1	747

SOLUTION

ROUND 162

LETTER GAME 1

A	Y	E	F	D	P	R	M	I

LETTER GAME 3

A	B	D	I	L	O	V	T	E

NUMBER GAME 1

25	8	8	6	4	5	383

CONUNDRUM

I	N	T	O	D	I	N	E	R

LETTER GAME 2

D	A	I	L	E	I	F	N	Z

LETTER GAME 4

G	R	Y	O	R	U	A	P	T

NUMBER GAME 2

7	7	5	5	3	3	444

SOLUTION

ROUND 163

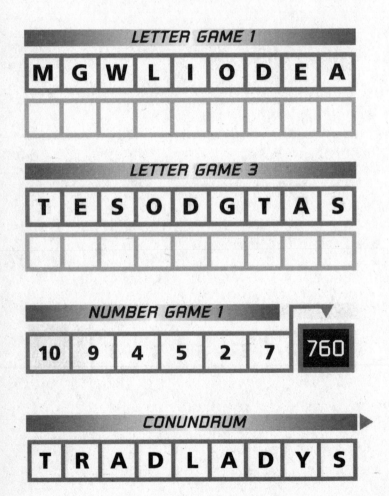

LETTER GAME 1

M	G	W	L	I	O	D	E	A

LETTER GAME 3

T	E	S	O	D	G	T	A	S

NUMBER GAME 1

10	9	4	5	2	7	760

CONUNDRUM

T	R	A	D	L	A	D	Y	S

LETTER GAME 2

P	A	O	R	T	X	H	S	E

LETTER GAME 4

E	S	Y	T	A	L	C	N	R

NUMBER GAME 2

75	25	50	6	7	9	665

SOLUTION

ROUND 164

LETTER GAME 1

E	D	R	I	T	G	F	U	R

LETTER GAME 3

N	E	V	I	O	L	B	O	I

NUMBER GAME 1

75	6	5	8	4	9	**951**

CONUNDRUM

B	L	A	M	E	G	O	L	D

LETTER GAME 2

T	A	R	E	P	O	C	H	N

LETTER GAME 4

T	S	L	E	A	I	B	O	P

NUMBER GAME 2

100	3	8	4	7	2	574

SOLUTION

ROUND 165

LETTER GAME 1

F	Y	S	Z	E	U	I	P	T

LETTER GAME 3

C	S	N	A	E	O	P	L	A

NUMBER GAME 1

25	3	7	2	4	5	980

CONUNDRUM

L	I	V	I	D	I	C	E	S

LETTER GAME 2

R	S	O	M	A	E	T	B	D

LETTER GAME 4

K	L	D	Y	T	E	A	E	C

NUMBER GAME 2

25	5	10	10	1	5	864

SOLUTION

ROUND 166

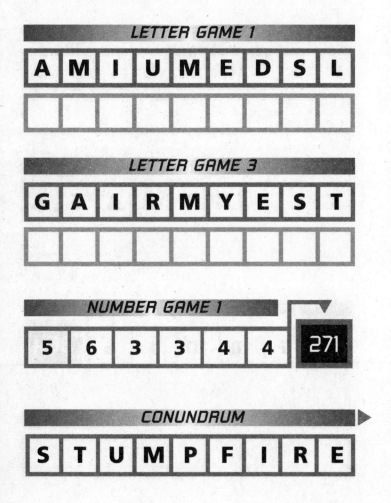

LETTER GAME 1

A	M	I	U	M	E	D	S	L

LETTER GAME 3

G	A	I	R	M	Y	E	S	T

NUMBER GAME 1

5	6	3	3	4	4	271

CONUNDRUM

S	T	U	M	P	F	I	R	E

LETTER GAME 2

A	S	C	T	O	R	V	R	E

LETTER GAME 4

Y	L	I	N	P	R	T	E	A

NUMBER GAME 2

75	2	7	1	10	6	347

SOLUTION

ROUND 167

LETTER GAME 1

O	D	R	Y	U	R	S	V	E

LETTER GAME 3

A	I	T	H	K	R	C	S	O

NUMBER GAME 1

50	25	75	6	5	7	**417**

CONUNDRUM

B	O	R	E	S	H	A	C	K

LETTER GAME 2

J	O	T	W	A	N	S	E	B

LETTER GAME 4

D	B	E	A	T	S	L	U	W

NUMBER GAME 2

50	5	4	3	1	3	801

SOLUTION

ROUND 168

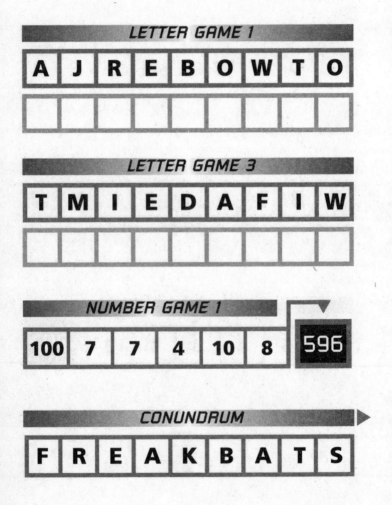

LETTER GAME 1

A	J	R	E	B	O	W	T	O

LETTER GAME 3

T	M	I	E	D	A	F	I	W

NUMBER GAME 1

100	7	7	4	10	8	596

CONUNDRUM

F	R	E	A	K	B	A	T	S

LETTER GAME 2

W	R	A	C	B	E	U	L	G

LETTER GAME 4

N	S	R	C	E	I	W	E	Y

NUMBER GAME 2

25	2	7	9	10	5	**992**

SOLUTION

ROUND 169

LETTER GAME 1

G	B	R	S	I	E	F	U	G

LETTER GAME 3

H	E	N	O	W	S	B	I	T

NUMBER GAME 1

75	50	6	8	4	9	**483**

CONUNDRUM

W	H	I	T	E	R	O	S	E

LETTER GAME 2

L	S	B	T	N	U	I	E	D

LETTER GAME 4

C	T	X	W	E	I	E	O	R

NUMBER GAME 2

50	8	3	5	8	1	756

SOLUTION

ROUND 170

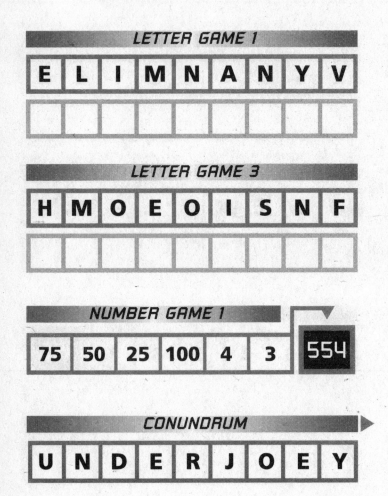

LETTER GAME 1

E	L	I	M	N	A	N	Y	V

LETTER GAME 3

H	M	O	E	O	I	S	N	F

NUMBER GAME 1

75	50	25	100	4	3	554

CONUNDRUM

U	N	D	E	R	J	O	E	Y

LETTER GAME 2

R	U	L	P	D	I	A	V	E

LETTER GAME 4

J	H	E	N	B	L	I	O	T

NUMBER GAME 2

100	4	7	8	1	6		288

SOLUTION

ROUND 171

LETTER GAME 1

N	S	M	E	U	C	O	E	P

LETTER GAME 3

N	R	L	U	E	O	Y	S	D

NUMBER GAME 1

75	100	8	4	2	6	**719**

CONUNDRUM

A	C	E	F	I	B	R	E	S

LETTER GAME 2

E	F	G	H	I	L	W	T	Y

LETTER GAME 4

O	K	R	Y	B	A	N	D	E

NUMBER GAME 2

100	1	1	2	2	3	927

SOLUTION

ROUND 172

LETTER GAME 1

W	P	O	D	L	E	T	Z	A

LETTER GAME 3

R	S	R	M	E	O	A	P	T

NUMBER GAME 1

25	5	9	9	8	7

469

CONUNDRUM

T	I	M	E	D	A	T	E	D

LETTER GAME 2

U	D	L	F	R	O	W	E	P

LETTER GAME 4

F	P	N	A	Y	O	L	M	E

NUMBER GAME 2

75	50	25	7	2	8	**530**

SOLUTION

T	R	I	G	N	O	M	I	T

ROUND 173

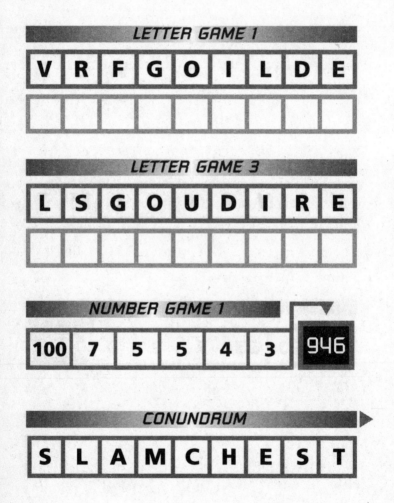

LETTER GAME 1

V	R	F	G	O	I	L	D	E

LETTER GAME 3

L	S	G	O	U	D	I	R	E

NUMBER GAME 1

100	7	5	5	4	3	946

CONUNDRUM

S	L	A	M	C	H	E	S	T

LETTER GAME 2

T	G	I	A	N	R	U	Y	A

LETTER GAME 4

H	L	V	R	A	O	E	M	T

NUMBER GAME 2

75	25	100	4	2	9	692

SOLUTION

ROUND 174

LETTER GAME 1

N	H	N	I	A	R	M	E	K

LETTER GAME 3

N	E	E	O	X	Y	T	A	G

NUMBER GAME 1

100	50	10	8	4	7	925

CONUNDRUM

P	O	L	A	R	A	N	E	E

LETTER GAME 2

P	Y	S	T	A	L	I	O	C

LETTER GAME 4

V	C	E	S	O	T	E	N	A

NUMBER GAME 2

25	7	3	1	5	9	666

SOLUTION

ROUND 175

LETTER GAME 1

O	C	D	U	Y	E	L	R	V

LETTER GAME 3

S	E	N	A	G	L	I	M	G

NUMBER GAME 1

50	100	2	4	5	6

749

CONUNDRUM

R	O	S	E	C	R	O	P	S

LETTER GAME 2

I	S	T	A	F	E	M	N	O

LETTER GAME 4

H	O	C	U	S	A	I	G	N

NUMBER GAME 2

25	1	6	4	2	5	**669**

SOLUTION

ROUND 176

LETTER GAME 1

H	U	B	E	A	S	R	D	N

LETTER GAME 3

N	L	E	U	C	A	R	E	L

NUMBER GAME 1

100	10	8	7	8	10	**246**

CONUNDRUM

E	A	R	T	H	C	L	A	D

LETTER GAME 2

G	Y	O	O	B	R	I	E	N

LETTER GAME 4

S	C	U	O	R	A	B	I	L

NUMBER GAME 2

25	8	7	2	2	4	888

SOLUTION

ROUND 177

LETTER GAME 1

K	I	H	A	D	E	V	S	E

LETTER GAME 3

O	B	L	A	D	I	M	Y	C

NUMBER GAME 1

25	1	6	8	9	1	**838**

CONUNDRUM

L	A	N	K	G	R	I	P	S

LETTER GAME 2

T	L	A	R	K	E	E	N	M

LETTER GAME 4

N	U	T	N	F	I	A	E	O

NUMBER GAME 2

25	8	10	4	6	2		824

SOLUTION

ROUND 178

LETTER GAME 1

E	R	D	M	I	N	A	O	Z

LETTER GAME 3

R	I	N	G	C	O	W	E	L

NUMBER GAME 1

50	75	9	1	3	4	**720**

CONUNDRUM

D	E	A	L	T	H	R	E	E

LETTER GAME 2

O	E	W	M	N	O	F	R	G

LETTER GAME 4

N	R	E	Y	A	B	T	O	N

NUMBER GAME 2

50	25	6	3	3	2		667

SOLUTION

ROUND 179

LETTER GAME 1

L	R	K	C	A	E	E	M	F

LETTER GAME 3

F	A	D	I	O	G	E	R	N

NUMBER GAME 1

25	6	2	3	4	4	**852**

CONUNDRUM

P	I	N	K	G	R	O	O	V

LETTER GAME 2

U	N	I	X	E	R	T	A	N

LETTER GAME 4

G	I	E	D	V	I	S	C	S

NUMBER GAME 2

25	2	3	5	7	9	887

SOLUTION

ROUND 180

LETTER GAME 1

O N I F E S H A D

LETTER GAME 3

V I R E S T E C E

NUMBER GAME 1

25 5 2 1 7 3 | 782

CONUNDRUM

N I N O R O U G H

LETTER GAME 2

S	I	N	C	D	R	E	E	E

LETTER GAME 4

C	R	I	D	T	E	M	I	H

NUMBER GAME 2

75	100	2	3	4	9	**844**

SOLUTION

ROUND 181

LETTER GAME 1

R	I	M	E	D	I	A	L	A

LETTER GAME 3

B	E	D	R	I	E	S	A	F

NUMBER GAME 1

75	5	3	6	8	4	**760**

CONUNDRUM

T	H	R	E	E	D	A	V	S

LETTER GAME 2

D	Y	P	O	L	E	M	E	R

LETTER GAME 4

A	R	R	I	P	D	E	E	H

NUMBER GAME 2

10	1	6	7	8	5	841

SOLUTION

ROUND 182

LETTER GAME 1

M	O	T	O	R	P	E	D	A

LETTER GAME 3

S	M	O	R	K	I	G	A	S

NUMBER GAME 1

100	25	7	4	1	8	**629**

CONUNDRUM

P	A	M	E	L	I	T	I	C

LETTER GAME 2

K	I	N	P	L	O	G	R	A

LETTER GAME 4

M	E	D	E	S	A	C	R	U

NUMBER GAME 2

25	50	8	3	7	5	**317**

SOLUTION

ROUND 183

LETTER GAME 1

S	U	P	T	E	D	A	L	F

LETTER GAME 3

F	R	A	C	T	E	R	A	E

NUMBER GAME 1

25	75	50	100	5	1

776

CONUNDRUM

M	A	C	A	R	O	N	I	P

LETTER GAME 2

V	I	R	B	U	S	O	T	E

LETTER GAME 4

P	O	A	L	E	J	A	N	W

NUMBER GAME 2

50	75	4	4	2	2	**776**

SOLUTION

ROUND 184

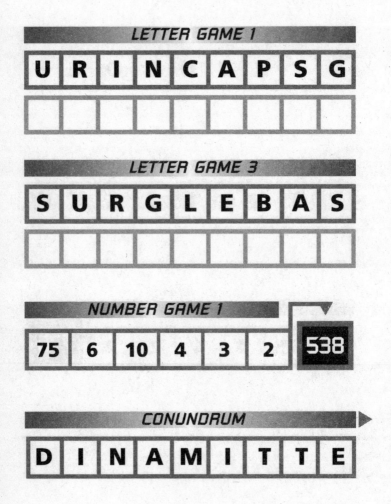

LETTER GAME 1

U	R	I	N	C	A	P	S	G

LETTER GAME 3

S	U	R	G	L	E	B	A	S

NUMBER GAME 1

75	6	10	4	3	2	538

CONUNDRUM

D	I	N	A	M	I	T	T	E

LETTER GAME 2

G	I	O	L	I	N	E	R	A

LETTER GAME 4

O	X	E	D	L	S	I	Y	C

NUMBER GAME 2

50	7	5	7	2	4	**820**

SOLUTION

ROUND 185

LETTER GAME 1

C	U	L	P	I	T	O	E	M

LETTER GAME 3

S	P	E	N	T	O	L	A	W

NUMBER GAME 1

25	75	100	8	9	10	**266**

CONUNDRUM

T	O	E	D	A	N	G	L	E

LETTER GAME 2

G	E	R	V	I	N	A	Q	U

LETTER GAME 4

R	I	G	U	T	I	S	T	A

NUMBER GAME 2

100	9	5	8	7	9	**643**

SOLUTION

ROUND 186

LETTER GAME 1

X	U	U	B	R	Y	P	E	A

LETTER GAME 3

B	L	U	F	E	T	A	R	E

NUMBER GAME 1

8	3	4	2	10	9	734

CONUNDRUM

A	N	O	I	N	T	E	S	S

LETTER GAME 2

C	H	E	A	R	U	P	S	C

LETTER GAME 4

P	E	L	B	K	E	A	E	R

NUMBER GAME 2

50	25	8	7	7	5	**543**

SOLUTION

ROUND 187

LETTER GAME 1

R	A	M	I	S	T	I	C	Y

LETTER GAME 3

O	C	B	T	R	A	I	A	E

NUMBER GAME 1

75	25	1	10	4	4	**841**

CONUNDRUM

M	A	G	I	C	T	R	A	P

LETTER GAME 2

N	I	F	A	N	C	E	R	E

LETTER GAME 4

C	O	D	I	M	A	G	T	U

NUMBER GAME 2

2	5	9	8	9	4	**570**

SOLUTION

ROUND 188

LETTER GAME 1

S	O	N	D	E	M	A	H	I

LETTER GAME 3

H	U	N	D	R	E	N	A	D

NUMBER GAME 1

25	2	3	8	3	6	**667**

CONUNDRUM

L	I	L	Y	Q	U	O	O	S

LETTER GAME 2

H	O	N	C	O	R	E	S	P

LETTER GAME 4

D	E	R	N	O	M	A	T	N

NUMBER GAME 2

25	75	100	10	10	9	**416**

SOLUTION

ROUND 189

LETTER GAME 1

D	I	N	R	E	E	T	S	K

LETTER GAME 3

D	E	L	B	U	R	E	N	A

NUMBER GAME 1

75	100	2	1	3	3	**936**

CONUNDRUM

R	A	C	I	E	T	E	X	T

LETTER GAME 2

C	O	N	E	J	A	T	D	K

LETTER GAME 4

T	H	O	R	O	S	P	A	C

NUMBER GAME 2

50	75	25	5	5	1	**386**

SOLUTION

ROUND 190

LETTER GAME 1

D	I	L	T	E	R	E	B	S

LETTER GAME 3

M	M	I	T	U	R	E	A	E

NUMBER GAME 1

100	7	10	9	10	1	**244**

CONUNDRUM

D	E	V	I	L	D	A	T	A

LETTER GAME 2

D	A	V	E	P	I	J	T	A

LETTER GAME 4

L	I	S	T	E	A	C	S	B

NUMBER GAME 2

25	75	50	100	8	7	**942**

SOLUTION

ROUND 191

Y	O	V	E	L	S	A	S	T

LETTER GAME 3

L	A	P	P	O	R	E	S	I

NUMBER GAME 1

9	4	3	7	5	2	999

CONUNDRUM

N	O	T	E	D	M	A	I	D

LETTER GAME 2

D	I	L	L	E	N	T	A	C

LETTER GAME 4

C	R	E	P	O	T	I	N	E

NUMBER GAME 2

25	100	7	7	4	3	**578**

SOLUTION

ROUND 192

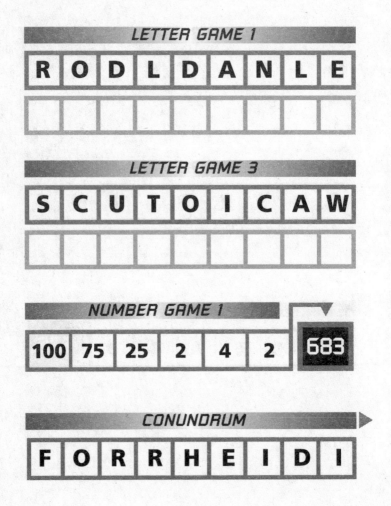

LETTER GAME 1

R	O	D	L	D	A	N	L	E

LETTER GAME 3

S	C	U	T	O	I	C	A	W

NUMBER GAME 1

100	75	25	2	4	2	683

CONUNDRUM

F	O	R	R	H	E	I	D	I

LETTER GAME 2

B	L	O	N	E	A	M	E	T

LETTER GAME 4

L	I	K	C	P	I	R	E	R

NUMBER GAME 2

50	100	1	10	10	1	**630**

SOLUTION

ROUND 193

D	R	U	I	I	F	E	P	F

LETTER GAME 3

A	N	I	G	E	R	D	A	T

NUMBER GAME 1

| 50 | 4 | 6 | 10 | 1 | 7 |

972

CONUNDRUM

G	R	A	N	D	P	I	N	E

402

LETTER GAME 2

A	R	R	W	E	D	R	A	T

LETTER GAME 4

R	E	C	S	T	O	O	E	S

NUMBER GAME 2

25	9	1	4	5	6	848

SOLUTION

ROUND 194

LETTER GAME 1

O	D	R	I	N	A	T	O	V

LETTER GAME 3

A	C	D	E	E	R	S	T	E

NUMBER GAME 1

50	25	75	3	1	2	**407**

CONUNDRUM

S	P	E	E	D	C	U	T	S

LETTER GAME 2

S	T	I	E	R	L	A	I	C

LETTER GAME 4

F	I	M	P	R	E	C	A	T

NUMBER GAME 2

50	25	9	2	5	7	828

SOLUTION

ROUND 195

H U D E M O S A I

M E T I L A C C A

| 75 | 5 | 1 | 6 | 6 | 1 | 542 |

P O N I P R O G S

LETTER GAME 2

F	O	O	L	B	H	E	K	S

LETTER GAME 4

S	L	I	T	M	A	N	A	W

NUMBER GAME 2

25	3	7	4	3	2	**882**

SOLUTION

ROUND 196

V	A	G	I	B	A	L	E	N

A	B	L	O	U	R	D	E	G

NUMBER GAME 1

2	8	4	5	4	1	**657**

CONUNDRUM

R	I	T	E	C	I	G	A	R

LETTER GAME 2

C	U	M	D	E	L	A	T	I

LETTER GAME 4

W	A	R	D	I	Y	E	V	J

NUMBER GAME 2

75	25	2	9	2	6		830

SOLUTION

ROUND 197

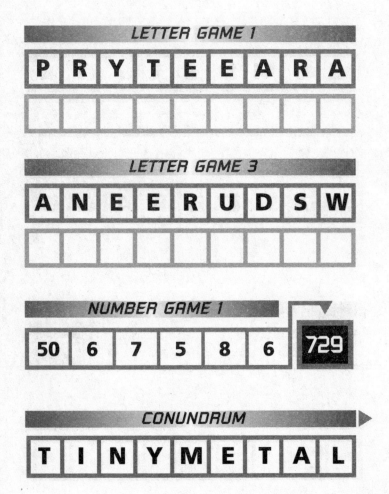

LETTER GAME 1

| P | R | Y | T | E | E | A | R | A |

LETTER GAME 3

| A | N | E | E | R | U | D | S | W |

NUMBER GAME 1

| 50 | 6 | 7 | 5 | 8 | 6 | 729 |

CONUNDRUM

| T | I | N | Y | M | E | T | A | L |

LETTER GAME 2

M	O	N	I	S	T	A	D	V

LETTER GAME 4

H	O	S	L	E	F	A	O	D

NUMBER GAME 2

50	25	8	2	7	10	**564**

SOLUTION

ROUND 198

LETTER GAME 1

G	E	L	T	A	I	A	T	P

LETTER GAME 3

I	H	B	E	N	S	T	A	L

NUMBER GAME 1

25	75	100	50	3	6	**429**

CONUNDRUM

N	E	C	K	B	L	A	D	E

LETTER GAME 2

D	R	O	K	E	B	N	W	A

LETTER GAME 4

G	I	N	E	R	S	T	A	X

NUMBER GAME 2

75	2	2	1	5	8	**695**

SOLUTION

413

ROUND 199

LETTER GAME 1

L	O	B	A	I	T	A	S	F

LETTER GAME 3

B	A	L	C	T	R	I	E	A

NUMBER GAME 1

100	25	9	4	4	8	956

CONUNDRUM

G	I	A	N	T	T	I	E	S

LETTER GAME 2

C	O	N	T	R	A	I	A	W

LETTER GAME 4

S	L	I	K	E	D	A	E	H

NUMBER GAME 2

25	10	6	6	3	1	**628**

SOLUTION

ROUND 200

R I N L I O N C E

B T I H E W T I A

| 7 | 6 | 3 | 3 | 8 | 2 | **591** |

O U R T E M P L E

LETTER GAME 2

H	A	R	G	L	I	N	E	O

LETTER GAME 4

T	I	S	E	L	I	N	W	A

NUMBER GAME 2

| 25 | 8 | 3 | 10 | 2 | 10 |

731

SOLUTION

Answers

Round 1

BLOCKAGES 9, BACKLOGS 8, LOCKAGE 7
DANDELION 9, ADENOID 7, LOADED 6
PLURALISE 9, PERUSAL 7, ALLURE 6
SAFEGUARD 9, SUGARED 7, GRADES 6
$(7 \times 25) - 3 = 172; 6 - (8 - 7) = 5; 172 \times 5 = 860$
$2 \times 9 \times 50 = 900; 2 \times 8 = 16; 900 + 16 = 916$
ADMIRABLE

Round 2

BACTERIA 8, ABREACT 7, CATERS 6
UNLOADED 8, DUODENA 7, NODULE 6
HAILSTONE 9, HOTLINES 8, ELATION 7
WAGONETTE 9, TENTAGE 7, GOATEE 6
$6 \times 100 = 600; 75 + 4 + 3 = 82; 600 + (2 \times 82) = 764$
$100 - (9 - 1) = 92; 92 \times 5 = 460; 460 + 10 - 1 = 469$
FORTIFIED

Round 3

NAARTJIE 8, KERATIN 7, RETAIN 6
OBELISK 7, BLOKES 6, SHEIK 5
UPSTAGED 8, GATEAUS 7, ADAPTS 6
DESCRIES 8, RESIDES 7, SLICES 6
$75 + 50 + (5 - 3) = 127; 127 \times 7 = 889; 889 + 25 = 914$
$9 \times 9 = 81; 81 + (6 - 4) = 83; (83 \times 10) + 3 = 833$
MASSAGING

Round 4

WINDPIPE 8, PAWNED, 6, WIPED 5
HAMBURGER 9, UMBRAGE 7, RHUMBA 6
SALESGIRL 9, GLASSIER 8, AIRLESS 7
CACOETHES 9, TEACHES 7, SCOTCH 6
$75 + 6 = 81; 8 - (50/25) = 6; 6 \times 81 = 486$
$2 \times 4 \times 25 = 200; 200 + 5 = 205; 205 \times 3 = 615$
VIOLINIST

Round 5

STATIONED 9, SEDATION 8, INSTEAD 7
VACCINATE 9, CAVATINE 8, VACCINE 7
RACEHORSE 9, RESEARCH 8, CAREERS 7
YARDAGE 7, DEARLY 6, GRAVE 5
$50 - 8 = 42; 42 \times 7 = 294; 294 - 3 = 291$
$75 + 7 + 5 = 87; 87 \times 6 = 522$
RETRACTED

Round 6

HANKERED 8, THANKED 7, ADHERE 6
SIGNATURE 9, URINATES 8, GRANITE 7
VULCANIZE 9, VINCULA 7, VENIAL 6
JACKPOTS 8, TOECAPS 7, POCKET 6
$(8 \times 4) + 3 = 35; 35 \times 25 = 875; 875 + 2 = 877$

$8 \times (50 - 6) = 352$; $352 - 5 = 347$
ENTAILING

Round 7

CRABMEAT 8, MACABRE 7, DREAMT 6
WALLOPED 8, TADPOLE 7, PALLET 6
CASUISTRY 9, SACRISTY 8, RACISTS 7
OUTNUMBER 9, BURNOUT 7, TUMOUR 6
$9 + 8 - 6 = 11$; $(75 + 11) \times 9 = 774$; $774 + 3 = 777$
$(5 + 3) \times 10 = 80$; $80 - (2/2) = 79$; $79 \times 6 = 474$
GENTLEMAN

Round 8

WAKENING 8, WEANING 7, OWNING 6
BAGATELLE 9, EATABLE 7, EAGLET 6
YUMMIEST 8, TUMMIES 7, MOIETY 6
BLACKOUT 8, OUTBACK 7, COBALT 6
$(9 \times 3) - 1 = 26$; $26 \times 25 = 650$; $650 + 4 + 1 = 655$
$7 \times (100/2) = 350$; $350 - (10 + 2) = 338$
UNFOUNDED

Round 9

UNPOPULAR 9, POPULAR 7, POPLAR 6
WOBBLIER 8, BLOWIER 7, RABBLE 6
CITYSCAPE 9, ASEPTIC 7, ACCEPT 6
CADAVERIC 9, AVARICE 7, CRAVED 6
$100 + 50 + (8/8) = 151$; $151 \times 5 = 755$; $755 + 4 = 759$
$75 + 25 - 7 = 93$; $93 \times 10 = 930$; $930 - 6 = 924$
SHADOWING

Round 10

STEADILY 8, IDEALLY 7, SLATED 6
MANOMETER 9, MEMENTO 7, MOMENT 6
ARYTENOID 9, RATIONED 8, DETRAIN 7
HAMPERED 8, EARTHED 7, PARTED 6
$25 + (5 \times 3) = 40$; $(40 + 2) \times 8 = 336$; $336 + 3 = 339$
$100 + (10 \times 10) = 200$; $200 + 9 + 7 = 216$
TRANSPORT

Round 11

LANKIEST 8, PANTILE 7, INLETS 6
BENTWOOD 8, BOOTED 6, TOWED 5
PICKETED 8, DEPICT 6, ADEPT 5
OBSCURANT 9, ROBUSTA 7, CARBON 6
$9 \times (8 + 4) = 108$; $(108 + 3) \times 8 = 888$
$(5 \times 75) - 5 = 370$; $(50/25) \times 370 = 740$
FESTOONED

Round 12

HARDWARE 8, HARRIED 7, DRAWER 6
SAMPHIRE 8, HAMPERS 7, PHRASE 6
VOLLEYING 9, LOVINGLY 8, YELLING 7
YARDBIRD 8, BRIARY 6, RABID 5
$(25 - 4) \times 8 = 168$; $168 + (50/10) = 173$
$(9 - 2) \times (100 - 4) = 672$; $672 - 1 = 671$
LADDERING

Round 13

CADENZA 7, FAÇADE 6, NAKED 5
RACKETING 9, REACTING 8, TRACING 7
KILOBYTE 8, LIBERTY 7, LOITER 6
WOMANIZED 9, WOMANIZE 8, MIAOWED 7
$(3 \times 10) + (6/3) = 32; 75 + 32 = 107; 107 \times 8 = 856$
$6 \times 75 = 450; 9 + (100/50) = 11; 450 + 11 = 461$
ISOLATION

Round 14

POLISHED 8, SPLODGE 7, SLEIGH 6
DAREDEVIL 9, DEADLIER 8, DELIVER 7
PILLOWED 8, WILLED 6, PLIED 5
BAILMENT 8, TIMBALE 7, NIMBLE 6
$100 + 25 + 1 = 126; 126 \times (6/2) = 378$
$4 \times 9 \times 25 = 900; 900 - (10 + 7) = 883$
REPUTABLE

Round 15

UNRELATED 9, UNDERATE 8, ALTERED 7
DEPARTING 9, GRADIENT 8, PAINTED 7
CALAMITY 8, ACTUAL 6, CLAIM 5
BUNFIGHT 8, FOUGHT 6, THING 5
$100 + 75 (2 \times 5) = 165; (165 \times 4) + 2 = 662$
$3 \times 4 \times 75 = 900; 900 - 100 = 800; 800 + 25 - 2 = 823$
FLICKERED

Round 16

RADIATOR 7, ADROIT 6, TARDY 5
SIxPENCE 8, SINCERE 7, ExPIRE 6
ENCAGES 7, ESCAPE 6, PECAN 5
FACSIMILE 9, FAMILIES 8, LAICISE 7
$(8 \times 75) - 50 = 550; 550 + 6 + 1 = 557$
$5 \times (7 + 1) = 40; 40 \times 25 = 1000; 1000 - (6 + 3) = 991$
TATTOOING

Round 17

PAGODAS 7, SEADOG 6, SPEAK 5
MACHISMO 8, CHAMOIS 7, MOSAIC 6
SURROGATE 9, OUTRAGES 8, TROUSER 7
CALUMNIES 9, MUSICALE 8, CAESIUM 7
$75 + 2 + 1 = 78; 78 \times 8 = 624; 624 + 50 = 674$
$(5 + 2) \times 2 = 14; 100 - 14 = 86; 86 \times 10 = 860; 860 - 3 = 857$
MOUTHWASH

Round 18

DARTBOARD 9, BARRATOR 8, ABROAD 6
YIELDING 8, DINGILY 7, INDIGO 6
EMIGRATED 9, DIAMETER 8, EMIRATE 7
VIRGATES 8, THRIVES 7, VISAGE 6
$(9 \times 7) - 3 = 60; (9 \times 60) - 4 = 536$
$(2 + 1) \times 25 = 75; (75 + 2) \times 10 = 770; 770 + 9 = 779$
AFTERLIFE

Round 19

WORRISOME 9, ROOMIER 7, SORROW 6
JAILBREAK 9, BALKIER 7, AERIAL 6
WARDROBE 8, BOARDER 7, ROARED 6

LISTABLE 8, LOBELIA 7, BALLOT 6
(3 − 1) × 50 = 100; (100 + 7) × (5 + 4) = 963
10 × 75 = 750; 750 − 100 − 50 = 600; 600 + 25 − 7 = 618
LUMBERING

Round 20

RAINCOAT 8, OCARINA 7, CARTON 6
BILINGUAL 9, BILLING 7, AILING 6
CAMSHAFT 8, MATCHES 7, ASTHMA 6
BUDGETARY 9, TRAGEDY 7, GRATED 6
100 + 25 − 2 = 123; 123 × 7 = 861; 861 − 1 = 860
(75 + 10) × 10 = 850; 6 + 5 + 3 = 14; 850 + 14 = 864
SHRINKAGE

Round 21

BOLDFACE 8, LOAFED 6, FLOOD 5
STEPSONS 8, PISTONS 7, STONES 6
OVERAWED 8, WATERED 7, TOWARD 6
POOLSIDE 8, SPOILED 7, POODLE 6
75 − (9/9) = 74; 6 × 74 = 444; 444 − 100 − 7 = 337
2 × (8 − 1) = 14; 14 × 50 = 700; 700 − (9 + 8) = 683
CORRODING

Round 22

CRABBY 6, CUBBY 5, ARIA 4
DATABASE 8, BASTARD 7, TREADS 6
YOUNGEST 8, IGNEOUS 7, GENIUS 6
BALLPOINT 9, PINBALL 7, OBTAIN 6
100 + 25 − (50/5) = 115; 115 × 8 = 920; 920 − 4 = 916
(2 × 75) − 6 = 144; 144 × 4 = 576; 576 − (2 + 1) = 573
TACKINESS

Round 23

EMBRYONIC 9, COMBINE 7, BONIER 6
UNCARING 8, RUINING 7, CURING 6
CANKEROUS 9, NACREOUS 8, CONKERS 7
TARGETING 9, TREATING 8, NITRATE 7
75 + 50 + 2 = 127; 127 × 7 = 889; 889 − (3 − 2) = 888
100 + 75 + 25 = 200; 9 − (50/10) = 4; 200 + 4 = 204
DETERGENT

Round 24

MACKEREL 8, MIRACLE 7, MALICE 6
FAMISHED 8, FISHED 6, SHEAF 5
LACEWORK 8, WARLOCK 7, CLERKS 6
LAMPOONED 9, LAMPOON 7, PLANED 6
(6 × 5) + 1 = 31; 31 × 25 = 775; 775 + 1 = 776
3 × 4 × 10 = 120; (120 + 7) × 5 = 635
RASPBERRY

Round 25

UNSALTED 8, SALUTED 7, JAUNTS 6
SCAVENGE 8, ENCAGES 7, AGENCY 6
CANTABILE 9, BALANCE 7, CLIENT 6
ANGLIEST 9, STEALING 8, GENITAL 7
75 − (4 + 2) = 69; 25 − (7 + 4) = 14; 69 × 14 = 966
8 × (7 + 1) = 64; 64 × (5 + 5) = 640; 640 + 2 = 642
MOTIVATED

Round 26

PALFREYS 8, PARSLEY 7, FLARES 6
NARCOTIC 8, ACTINIC 7, RATION 6
BALCONIES 9, SOCIABLE 8, SANICLE 7
OBSIDIAN 8, IONISED 7, ANODES 6
$10 \times 9 \times 7 = 630$; $630 + 100 + 10 + 1 = 741$
$9 + (8/2) = 13$; $13 \times 50 = 650$; $650 + 6 = 656$
PREACHING

Round 27

BROTHER 7, AUTHOR 6, BERTH 5
VINTAGERS 9, ANGRIEST 8, STRIVEN 7
CAPSIZED 8, SPICED 6, SEPIA 5
SIZEABLE 8, BALDIES 7, SEALED 6
$(9 \times 50) + 75 = 525$; $(100/25) - 1 = 3$; $525 - 3 = 522$
$8 \times 5 = 40$; $40 \times (75/3) = 1000$; $1000 - 1 = 999$
EFFICIENT

Round 28

VINDALOO 8, OVATION 7, LOTION 6
HEADGEAR 8, DRAGEE 6, RAGED 5
ZESTIEST 8, EASIEST 7, SIESTA 6
ARROGANT 8, NARRATE 7, RANGER 6
$(10 + 5) \times 50 = 750$; $750 - (25 + 2) = 723$
$100 + 5 + 3 = 108$; $108 \times (9 - 3) = 648$
ALBATROSS

Round 29

ELOQUENT 8, TOLUENE 7, ELUENT 6
SCHIZOID 8, IODIZES 7, COSHED 6
VALENTINE 9, VENETIAN 8, ENLIVEN 7
CAPTIONED 9, PEDANTIC 8, NOTEPAD 7
$2 \times 9 \times 50 = 900$; $(9 - 4) \times 7 = 35$; $900 - 35 = 865$
$(75 + 4) \times 10 = 790$; $100/50 = 2$; $790 - (6/2) = 787$
MONKEYING

Round 30

PORTRAIT 8, AIRPORT 7, ROTTER 6
MAGAZINE 8, MANAGED 7, MAIDEN 6
STILETTO 8, THISTLE 7, TOILET 6
BRITCHES 8, BRIOCHE 7, CHORES 6
$(100/4) + 1 = 26$; $26 \times 9 = 234$
$4 \times (3 + 1) = 16$; $16 \times (25 + 2) = 432$; $432 - 1 = 431$
UNDAMAGED

Round 31

UNAWARES 8, UNSCREW 7, ANSWER 6
WATERBED 8, BERATED 7, TIRADE 6
JAVELINS 8, NAIVELY 7, SALINE 6
RATEPAYER 9, TAPERER 7, ERRATA 6
$(100 - 9) \times 8 = 728$; $728 - 50 = 678$; $678 - (4/4) = 677$
$75 - (8 + 4) = 63$; $63 \times 3 = 189$; $189 \times 5 = 945$
RECEPTION

Round 32

UNCLIMBED 9, INCLUDE 7, INDUCE 6
HERALDIC 8, RECITAL 7, TRACED 6
UNWANTED 8, TWANGED 7, GNAWED 6

DEBACLES 8, BEAGLES 7, SLEDGE 6
100 + 7 + (6/2) = 110; 110 × (7 + 1) = 880
(75 + 6) × 9 = 729; 729 − 5 = 724
IMPASSIVE

Round 33

NARROWEST 9, SENATOR 7, ARROWS 6
COMPENDIA 9, PANDEMIC 8, NOMADIC 7
CAPTIVATE 9, ACTIVATE 8, CAPTIVE 7
ELEPHANT 8, PLEATED 7, PEAHEN 6
9 × 9 = 81; (8 + 3) × 81 = 891; 891 + 8 + 7 = 906
(7 + 5) × (50 + 4) = 648; 648 − (5 + 4) = 639
TENDERING

Round 34

BANISHED 8, BEHINDS 7, WIDENS 6
STEVEDORE 9, DEVOTEES 8, DESERVE 7
FATEFUL 7, FAULTS 6, STUFF 5
FAREWELL 8, WELFARE 7, FILLER 6
10 + 10 + 2 = 22; 22 × 25 = 550; 550 + (6 × 4) = 574
(7 + 3) × 100 = 1000; (75/5) × 3 = 45; 1000 − 45 = 955
LANDSLIDE

Round 35

SCORPION 8, OPSONIC 7, CROONS 6
BRIEFCASE 9, FREESIA 7, FIBRES 6
MAILBOXES 9, MIXABLE 7, MOBILE 6
CARDAMOM 8, COMRADE 7, ARCADE 6
75 − 8 = 67; 67 − (50/25) = 65; 65 × 8 = 520; 520 + 100 = 620
(3 × 9) + 4 = 31; 31 × 25 = 775; 775 + 10 = 785
ASPARAGUS

Round 36

WAXCLOTH 8, LOCATE 6, CHEAT 5
ARCHIVED 8, RAWHIDE 7, CRAVED 6
ZOMBIFY 7, OPIUM 5, BUMP 4
MEDICATE 8, DICTATE 7, MATTED 6
50 + 25 − (10 − 9) = 74; (9 + 2) × 74 = 814
100 + 75 + 50 = 225; 9 + 9 + 6 = 24; 225 + 24 = 249
WHOLESOME

Round 37

OBSTETRIC 9, BISECTOR 8, BITTERS 7
PANDERING 9, REAPING 7, GARDEN 6
PASTILLE 8, ESTIVAL 7, PLATES 6
TAXIDERMY 9, DAYTIME 7, DREAMY 6
(3 × 25) + 5 = 80; (6 × 80) + 4 = 484
(8 × 50) + 100 = 500; 25 + 7 − 2 = 30; 500 + 30 = 530
SIMILARLY

Round 38

LARCENIES 9, SILENCER 8, CLEANSE 7
PROUDEST 8, GROUTED 7, TOURED 6
HEXASTYLE 9, EYELASH 7, EXALTS 6
SKINHEAD 8, SARDINE 7, SINKER 6
(8 × 10) + 6 = 86; 9 − (2 + 1) = 6; 86 × 6 = 516
75 + 3 = 78; 78 × 9 = 702
MULTIPLEX

Round 39

BANISTER 8, REPAINT 7, BRAINS 6
UKULELE 7, CUPULE 6, PLUCK 5
VAMPIRES 8, WAIVERS 7, ASPIRE 6
WAKENING 8, DAWNING 7, WINKED 6
$100 - 2 = 98; 98 \times (4 \times 2) = 784; 784 + 75 = 859$
$6 \times 75 = 450; 25 - (100/50) = 23; 450 - 23 = 427$
RECEIVING

Round 40

CASHBACK 8, CHICKS 6, BASIC 5
NASTINESS 9, SESTINAS 8, SIESTAS 7
PASTURED 8, TRAIPSE 7, PARTED 6
BANTERING 9, REBATING 8, NEARING 7
$(6 + 4 + 3) \times 50 = 650; 650 + (9 \times 9) = 731$
$25 + 6 + 2 = 33; 33 \times 3 \times 10 = 990$
PROPRIETY

Round 41

MAKEOVER 8, REMOVED 7, MARKED 6
DECIPHER 8, PREDICT 7, RECIPE 6
SCREWBALL 9, WARBLES 7, LABELS 6
STOCKIEST 9, STOCKIST 8, TICKETS 7
$(50 + 9) \times 3 = 177; 177 - (7 - 4) = 174; 174 \times 5 = 870$
$(6 \times 50) + 100 = 400; 400 - (9 - 2) = 393$
WAISTBAND

Round 42

CEASEFIRE 9, FRICASEE 8, FIACRES 7
MUTILATE 8, GIMLET 6, AGLET 5
REALISTIC 9, ARTICLES 8, REALIST 7
ELASTOMER 9, MOLESTER 8, REMOTES 7
$4 \times 4 \times 5 = 80; 9 \times 80 = 720; 720 + (6 - 5) = 721$
$7 \times 6 \times 2 = 84; 5 \times (3 - 1) = 10; 84 \times 10 = 840$
HYPERBOLE

Round 43

VILLAGER 8, ALLEGRO 7, GRAVEL 6
BREASTFED 9, BREASTED 8, DEAREST 7
UNCOUTHLY 9, UNCOUTH 7, TOUCHY 6
HINDRANCE 9, INARCHED 8, HANDIER 7
$3 \times 8 \times 25 = 600; 2 \times 3 \times 9 = 54; 600 + 54 = 654$
$8 \times 7 = 56; 100 - (75 + 10) = 15; (56 - 15) \times 9 = 369$
LABORIOUS

Round 44

CELESTIAL 9, ELASTIC 7, CLEATS 6
PARACHUTE 9, CAPTURE 7, TEACUP 6
SURFACED 8, TRADUCE 7, CRATED 6
GRAFTING 8, RAFTING 7, FRIGHT 6
$(2 \times 50) - 1 = 99; 99 \times (7 + 3) = 990; 990 + 2 = 992$
$(100 + 25) \times 6 = 750; 8 - (4/4) = 7; 750 + 7 = 757$
AFFECTION

Round 45

OCARINAS 8, INSOFAR 7, CASINO 6
DENIGRATE 9, TREADING 8, GRENADE 7
OPERATICS 9, PRACTISE 8, SEAPORT 7

TEASPOON 8, TOECAPS 7, OCTANE 6
$10 \times (50 - 1) = 490; 490 + (75/25) = 493; 493 - 100 = 393$
$9 \times 50 = 450; 450 - (75/25) = 447; 447 \times (8/4) = 894$
LOOSENING

Round 46

JEROBOAM 8, BROMATE 7, REBOOT 6
STOMACHED 9, HEADMOST 8, CATHODE 7
CHAGRINED 9, REACHING 8, CRINGED 7
UFOLOGIST 9, OLOGIST 7, FLOUTS 6
$(2 \times 7) + 4 = 18; 18 \times 50 = 900; 900 + (8 \times 3) = 924$
$8 - (10 - 9) = 7; 7 \times 75 = 525; 525 + 4 = 529$
BRAINWAVE

Round 47

BREADLINE 9, DENIABLE 8, BRINDLE 7
HONEYDEW 8, HONEYED 7, ANYHOW 6
EMULSIFY 8, HIMSELF 7, HELIUM 6
BAREFACED 9, REFACED 7, ARCADE 6
$(5 + 6) - (1 + 1) = 9; 9 \times (100 - 7) = 837$
$4 - (2/2) = 3; 3 \times 9 \times 25 = 675; 675 - 4 = 671$
IMPERFECT

Round 48

AUSTERITY 9, ESTUARY 7, STATUE 6
BABYSIT 7, ABBOTS 6, TABBY 5
OVERPRICE 9, OVERRIPE 8, RECOVER 7
GROUPIES 8, PIROGUE 7, GROPES 6
$6 \times 5 = 30; 30 \times (25 + 1) = 780; 780 + 4 - 1 = 783$
$7 \times (100 - 8) = 644; (50/5) +10 = 20; 644 - 20 = 624$
MARKETING

Round 49

PASTRAMI 8, IMPORTS 7, RAPIST 6
PAGANISE 8, AGONISE 7, PONIES 6
STEAMROLL 9, MAESTRO 7, TALLER 6
CALIBRATE 9, BACTERIA 8, CABARET 7
$75 + 2 = 77; (6 + 1) \times 77 = 539; 539 + 9 = 548$
$100 + 75 + 25 = 200; (200 - 6) \times 4 = 776; 776 + 50 = 826$
TIGHTENED

Round 50

WESTBOUND 9, SNOUTED 7, DEBUTS 6
ZEALOTRY 8, EATERY 6, EARLY 5
EARBASHED 9, BEHEADS 7, ERASED 6
STAIRWELL 9, LITERALS 8, RETAILS 7
$(8 + 5) \times 50 = 650; (9 \times 2) - 1 = 17; 650 - 17 = 633$
$(9 + 7) \times 25 = 400; 100 - (8 \times 7) = 44; 400 + 44 = 444$
COLLECTOR

Round 51

SQUIREDOM 9, SQUIRMED 8, MOUSIER 7
CARPENTER 9, RECREANT 8, CATERER 7
YABBERING 9, BRAYING 7, REGAIN 6
YEARBOOK 8, BAKERY 6, BROKE 5
$9 \times (50 + 25) = 675; 675 + 9 + 2 = 686; 686 + 100 = 786$
$10 + 2 + 1 = 13; 13 \times (50 + 2) = 676$
BUTTONING

Round 52

DEXTERITY 9, EXITED 6, TRIED 5
AROMATIC 8, MARITAL 7, COITAL 6
PAINTWORK 9, PATRON 6, PRANK 5
SQUELCHY 8, CLIQUES 7, CHISEL 6
$7 \times 8 \times 10 = 560$; $560 - (4 + 1) = 555$
$6/ (7 - 5) = 3$; $(9 \times 10) + 3 = 93$; $93 \times 8 = 744$
DISPLACED

Round 53

FOOLHARDY 9, LOOFAH 6, FLOOD 5
CARTILAGE 9, TRAGICAL 8, ARTICLE 7
TYPEFACE 8, PREFACE 7, CARPET 6
WATERHOLE 9, WEATHER 7, LOATHE 6
$75 - (50/25) = 73$; $73 \times 8 = 584$; $584 + 100 + 3 = 687$
$(7 \times 5) \times 25 = 875$; $875 + (9 - 8) = 876$
PURPORTED

Round 54

PALMTOPS 8, LAPTOPS 7, ALMOST 6
WINEMAKER 9, RAMEKIN 7, MARINE 6
GOSSAMER 8, MAESTRO 7, STORES 6
ARACHNID 8, RADIANT 7, RANCID 6
$(5 + 4) \times (100 + 2) = 918$; $918 + 10 + 3 = 931$
$75 + (50/25) = 77$; $3 \times (2 + 1) = 9$; $9 \times 77 = 693$
LOITERING

Round 55

SPREADING 9, READINGS 8, PRANGED 7
HOSPITAL 8, ASPHALT 7, POSTAL 6
TRIUMPHED 9, THUMPED 7, UMPIRE 6
CARETAKER 9, RETRACE 7, CREATE 6
$(50 + 5) \times 2 = 110$; $(110 \times 9) - 2 = 988$
$50 + 6 + 4 = 60$; $(8 + 5) \times 60 = 780$; $780 - 8 = 772$
LOCKSMITH

Round 56

WEBMASTER 9, BERATES 7, BEWARE 6
SPECIFIC 8, SCEPTIC 7, CITIES 6
BARNACLE 8, BALANCE 7, CLARET 6
WASSAILED 9, ASSAILED 8, ALIASES 7
$75 + 9 = 84$; $(6 + 4) \times 84 = 840$
$3 \times (4 + 1) = 15$; $15 \times 25 = 375$; $375 - (7 + 2) = 366$
TREMBLING

Round 57

GLYCERINE 9, REGENCY 7, LINGER 6
BULLETINS 9, UTENSIL 7, BLUEST 6
RULERSHIP 9, PLUSHIER 8, HURRIES 7
SPACEMAN 8, PANCAKE 7, SEAMAN 6
$7 \times 75 = 525$; $9 + 8 - 3 = 14$; $525 - 14 = 511$
$(4 \times 10) \times (4 \times 5) = 800$; $800 + (7 \times 5) = 835$
INVISIBLE

Round 58

FLEXITIME 9, LIFETIME 8, LEFTIE 6
TREATMENT 9, ENTREAT 7, MATTER 6
MUTILATES 9, SIMULATE 8, AMULETS 7

LOWERMOST 9, TREMOLOS 8, LOOTERS 7
75 + 9 + 8 = 92; (92 × 10) + 9 = 929
8 × (100 − 7) = 744; 75/25 = 3; 744 − (3/3) = 743
SOLDIERED

Round 59

WARHORSE 8, SPARROW 7, PHASER 6
OVERTAXED 9, OVEREAT 7, ADVERT 6
WAREHOUSE 9, REHOUSE 7, SHOWER 6
CARDPHONE 9, ANCHORED 8, PARCHED 7
2 × 3 × 6 = 36; (36 − 2) × 25 = 850; 850 + 4 = 854
10 × 10 = 100; 100 + (100/50) = 102; (75/25) × 102 = 306
ANIMOSITY

Round 60

MOTORCADE 9, DEMOCRAT 8, REDCOAT 7
PUCCOONS 8, COUPONS 7, CUCKOO 6
CAUTERIZE 9, AZURITE 7, CREATE 6
BALLPOINT 9, PINBALL 7, OBTAIN 6
(8 + 5) × 75 = 975; (8 × 4) + 10 = 42; 975 − 42 = 933
9 × (50 + 7) = 513; 513 + 8 = 521
ORDAINING

Round 61

TRANSPIRE 9, TERRAPIN 8, PAINTER 7
AMPOULES 8, MALTOSE 7, PLATES 6
VULTURES 8, RIVULET 7, SILVER 6
DETOXIFY 8, EXOTIC 6, FIXED 5
25 − (5 − 3) = 23; 10 + 8 = 18; 18 × 23 = 414
7 × (10 + 2) = 84; 4 + 4 = 8; 84 × 8 = 672
SHABBIEST

Round 62

COUPLETS 8, POSTURE 7, CLOUTS 6
BANQUETED 9, EQUATED 7, BEATEN 6
HOOLIGAN 8, HOWLING 7, LOWING 6
PARAGLIDE 9, REGALIA 7, GLIDER 6
(2 × 50) − 4 = 96; 96 × 10 = 960; 960 + (5 + 2) = 967
100 + 7 + 5 =112; (6 + 1) × 112 = 784; 784 + 75 = 859
THUNDERED

Round 63

VOYAGEUR 8, FORGAVE 7, VOYEUR 6
PARBOILED 9, PIEBALD 7, PAROLE 6
LOTTERIES 9, RETITLES 8, LOITERS 7
SOMBRERO 8, ROOSTER 7, MOTORS 6
(50 + 4) × 2 = 108; (108 + 3) × 9 = 999
6 + (75/25) = 9; 9 × 8 = 72; 100 + 72 + 50 = 222
CORKSCREW

Round 64

SOFTBACK 8, SETBACK 7, FACETS 6
PASTURED 8, PARQUET 7, QUARTS 6
TRADESMAN 9, MANDATES 8, MANTRAS 7
MORPHINE 8, MONIKER 7, HEROIN 6
100 − (7 + 5) = 88; 88 × 7 = 616
(4 × 25) + 3 = 103; (4 + 2) × 103 = 618; 618 + 1 = 619
TIPTOEING

Round 65

SOBRIQUET 9, BRIQUETS 8, BUSTIER 7
VOICEMAIL 9, ALCOVE 6, CLAIM 5
BEARSKIN 8, ARSENIC 7, BICKER 6
FLAMINGO 8, PALMING 7, MALIGN 6
$(7 \times 5) + 3 = 38; (50 + 38) \times 10 = 880; 880 - 4 = 876$
$(3 \times 4) + 1 = 13; 13 \times (8 \times 5) = 520; 520 + 2 = 522$
HEARTBEAT

Round 66

SNOWFALL 8, SWOLLEN 7, FALLEN 6
BARGEPOLE 9, OPERABLE 8, PERGOLA 7
CARNOTITE 9, REACTION 8, CATTIER 7
TOWELING 8, TOWLINE 7, TWINGE 6
$9 \times 75 = 675; 675 + 100 + 6 = 781$
$100 - (9 - 2) = 93; 93 \times 10 = 930; 930 + 2 + 1 = 933$
SPREADING

Round 67

MOONSCAPE 9, COMPOSE 7, POMACE 6
WHORLING 8, HOWLING 7, GLORIA 6
ONLOOKERS 9, SNORKEL 7, SOONER 6
OVULATING 9, VAULTING 8, ANTILOG 7
$6 \times (5 - 3) = 12; 12 \times (75 - 4) = 852; 852 - 50 = 802$
$(7 + 2) \times 25 = 225; (225 - 10) \times 3 = 645$
MESMERISE

Round 68

TORNADOES 9, RATOONED 8, SNORTED 7
SNARLING 8, SOARING 7, ORGANS 6
CERTAINTY 9, INTERACT 8, CATTERY 7
SOLITARY 8, TAILORS 7, STRAIT 6
$75 + (100/50) = 77; 77 \times 4 = 308; 308 - 25 = 283$
$75 + 2 + 2 + 1 = 80; 4 \times 3 \times 80 = 960$
PERSUADED

Round 69

PEDALOES 8, PLEASED 7, BLADES 6
SMOOCHED 8, MEDICOS 7, CHOOSE 6
BUMPINESS 9, NIMBUSES 8, MINUSES 7
ANEURYSM 8, SURNAME 7, MANURE 6
$3 \times (25 + 9) = 102; 102 \times 6 = 612; 612 - (6 - 5) = 611$
$(50 - 10) \times 8 = 320; 320 + 3 - 4 = 319$
CHASTISED

Round 70

ISSUANCE 8, CRUISES 7, CRANES 6
WANDERED 8, WARDEN 6, DRAWN 5
CUSPIDATE 9, AUSPICE 7, SPACED 6
MODULATE 8, MOULTED 7, LOQUAT 6
$(8 \times 10) + 10 = 90; (7 \times 90) - 9 = 621$
$25 + 4 - 9 = 20; 20 \times 50 = 1000; 1000 - 2 = 998$
PONDEROUS

Round 71

CAPSULATE 9, PLACATES 8, TEACUPS 7
PEEKABOO 8, POOKA 5, BOOK 4
DOMINOES 8, GOODIES 7, DENIMS 6

MINEFIELD 9, INFIDEL 7, DEFINE 6
100 + 10 + 2 = 112; (5 + 2) × 112 = 784
(10 + 2) × 9 = 108; 108 + 25 = 133; 133 × 7 = 931
PATTERING

Round 72

HIBERNATE 9, TRAINEE 7, BREATH 6
THUMBNAIL 9, HALIBUT 7, LABIUM 6
BARRISTER 9, BARRIERS 8, RAREBIT 7
ADOPTED 7, PADDLE 6, BLOAT 5
(75/25) × 3 = 9; 100 − (1 + 1) = 98; 98 × 9 = 882
6 × (50 + 2) = 312; 312 + 100 + 9 = 421
ALLOCATED

Round 73

PENALISE 8, PELICAN 7, SPLICE 6
ANYTHING 8, INANITY 7, HATING 6
CHAMPION 8, CAMPION 7, PHONIC 6
OWNERSHIP 9, WHISPER 7, HERONS 6
8 + 6 = 14; 14 × (75 − 4) = 994; 994 + (10/2) = 999
(3 × 50) − 9 = 141; (10/2) × 141 = 705; 705 + 1 = 706
BLANKETED

Round 74

ADVISOR 7, LIZARD 6, AVOID 5
METHADONE 9, ANTHEMED 8, METHANE 7
BRAINWAVE 9, WAIVER 6, BRINE 5
OPTICAL 7, POSTAL 6, CLAWS 5
(8 + 7) × 10 = 150; (150 + 1) × 6 = 906; 906 + 3 = 909
100 + 50 + 8 = 158; 158 × 4 = 632; 632 + 3 − 1 = 634
ANIMATION

Round 75

PENTHOUSE 9, ENTHUSE 7, POTEEN 6
CUFFLINK 8, UNCIAL 6, FLANK 5
BATHROOM 8, ROWBOAT 7, WOMBAT 6
URBANISED 9, BRANDIES 8, BRAINED 7
(10 × 10) + 9 = 109; (75/25) × 109 = 327; 327 + 50 = 377
9 × 4 × 25 = 900; 7 × (9 − 3) = 42; 900 − 42 = 858
INHABITED

Round 76

SKELETAL 8, OLEATES 7, ALLOTS 6
THINGAMY 8, ANYTIME 7, HATING 6
EROTICISM 9, MORTICES 8, MOISTER 7
BAYONETED 9, BAYONET 7, DENOTE 6
2 × 100 = 200; 200 + 25 − 5 = 220; 220 × 4 = 880
10 − 2 = 8; 8 × 5 × 10 = 400; 400 + 75 − 7 = 468
CAROUSING

Round 77

ANCHOVIES 9, EVASION 7, CHIVES 6
ELUCIDATE 9, DELICATE 8, DIALECT 7
SINCERITY 9, INCITERS 8, CISTERN 7
GINORMOUS 9, GUNROOMS 8, MOORING 7
5 + 4 + 4 = 13; 100 + 50 − 13 = 137; 137 × 5 = 685
5 + 7 − 3 = 9; 9 × (75 − 1) = 666
ASTRONOMY

Round 78

PHILANDER 9, HELIPAD 7, HINDER 6
ROULETTE 8, LETTER 6, OUTER 5
KNOWLEDGE 9, GOLDEN 6, WEDGE 5
THEORISES 9, SHORTIES 8, STEREOS 7
$8 - (5 - 3) = 6$; $6 \times 75 = 450$; $450 - 9 = 441$
$(7 + 4) \times 25 = 275$; $(275 + 1) \times 3 = 828$; $828 + 2 = 830$
BECKONING

Round 79

BICONCAVE 9, VACCINE 7, BOVINE 6
AMETHYST 8, STEAMY 6, MATHS 5
BEANFEAST 9, ABSENT 6, FATES 5
OPTIMIZE 8, EPIZOIC 7, POETIC 6
$(4 \times 6) - (2/2) = 23$; $(8 \times 100) - 23 = 777$
$(10 \times 10) - 7 = 93$; $93 \times 9 = 837$; $837 + 5 = 842$
WEARISOME

Round 80

CANOODLE 8, CONDOLE 7, CLONED 6
INVASION 8, SAPONIN 7, PIANOS 6
PHOSPHATE 9, PATHOS 6, HATES 5
FETLOCKS 8, TICKLES 7, FLECKS 6
$(50 + 25) \times 2 = 150$; $150 - (8 + 1) = 141$; $141 \times 7 = 987$
$100 + 9 + 4 = 113$; $113 \times 6 = 678$
DELEGATED

Round 81

JINGOISM 8, AMIGOS 6, GAINS 5
TURBINES 8, BRUISED 7, RUSTED 6
BECHAMEL 8, BLEACH 6, BLAZE 5
CHELATION 9, CHATLINE 8, ETHICAL 7
$(100 + 75) \times 3 = 525$; $525 + 3 = 528$; $528 + (50/25) = 530$
$50 + 25 + 7 = 82$; $82 \times 4 = 328$; $328 + 5 = 333$
ENJOYABLE

Round 82

PIPETTES 8, SPITTLE 7, TITLES 6
HEARTSICK 9, CHARIEST 8, STICKER 7
LIMOUSINE 9, EMULSION 8, ELUSION 7
BEDSPREAD 9, SPEARED 7, SADDER 6
$75 + 25 - 5 = 95$; $95 \times 7 = 665$; $665 - (3 + 3) = 659$
$(7 + 5) \times 25 = 300$; $300 + (7 \times 6) = 342$
INTRUSION

Round 83

BELLYACHE 9, EYEBALL 7, BLEACH 6
DEFAULTED 9, DEFLATED 8, DELATED 7
SHUFFLED 8, FLUSHED 7, FLUIDS 6
NOSTALGIC 9, COASTING 8, LASTING 7
$7 + 7 + 3 = 17$; $17 \times (50 - 1) = 833$; $833 - 6 = 827$
$50 - (4 + 4) = 42$; $42 \times 8 = 336$; $336 - (6/2) = 333$
PENETRATE

Round 84

CONVULSE 8, LOUNGES 7, UNCLES 6
SWEATSHOP 9, POSHEST 7, PATHOS 6
PISCATORY 9, APRICOTS 8, PROSAIC 7

METAFILE 8, MALEATE 7, FEMALE 6
$9 \times (75 + 5) = 720; 720 + (100/25) = 724$
$(75 - 2) \times 8 = 584; 100 + 25 - 10 = 115; 584 - 115 = 469$
INFESTING

Round 85

SHOEBLACK 9, BACKHOES 8, SHACKLE 7
ROLLMOP 7, IMPORT 6, TRILL 5
LIGHTENED 9, DELETING 8, DELIGHT 7
BROACHED 8, TORCHED 7, COATED 6
$(2 \times 7) + 4 = 18; 18 \times 50 = 900; 900 + 25 + 9 = 934$
$(9 \times 8) - 1 = 71; 71 \times 10 = 710; 710/2 = 355$
WORRISOME

Round 86

BROWBEAT 8, PROBATE 7, BOATER 6
JETLINER 8, THEREIN 7, ENTIRE 6
ONCOMING 8, AWAITED 7, INMATE 6
UNBEATEN 8, PENNATE 7, BUTANE 6
$(8 \times 8) - 5 = 59; 7 + 3 + 2 = 12; 12 \times 59 = 708$
$3 \times (7 - 1) = 18; 18 \times 25 = 450; 450 - (5 + 1) = 444$
GUTTERING

Round 87

RIDERSHIP 9, DISHIER 7, SPIDER 6
KNITWEAR 8, RETRAIN 7, WANKER 6
CLASSMATE 9, CALMEST 7, CAMELS 6
STATEMENT 9, TESTATE 7, ATTEST 6
$(8 \times 100) - 25 = 775; (2 \times 8) + 10 = 26; 775 - 26 = 749$
$3 \times 9 \times 25 = 675; (8 \times 6) - 1 = 47; 675 + 47 = 722$
CONCEITED

Round 88

OILFIELD 8, FILLED 6, PILED 5
AMBERGRIS 9, ARMIGERS 8, MARRIES 7
NOSEBAND 8, BONNIES 7, ANODES 6
SHIRTIEST 9, THIRTIES 8, HITTERS 7
$7 \times 7 = 49; 49 - (8 - 6) = 47; 8 \times 47 = 376$
$75 + 8 = 83; 83 \times 6 \times 2 = 996; 996 - 3 = 993$
CORDIALLY

Round 89

MAVERICK 8, TACKIER 7, ACTIVE 6
CINEPLEX 8, RECLINE 7, PINCER 6
AVERSION 8, INSHORE 7, HEROIN 6
PUBLICAN 8, UNCIAL 6, QUAIL 5
$(9 - 7) \times 75 = 150; 150 + 100 - 8 = 242$
$3 \times 3 \times (2 + 1) = 27; 27 \times (25 - 1) = 648$
BIOGRAPHY

Round 90

QUICKSTEP 9, QUICKEST 8, PIQUETS 7
SHAMROCK 8, MARCHES 7, HACKER 6
LEMONADE 8, OMENTAL 7, LAMENT 6
DYSPHORIA 9, SHIPYARD 8, HAIRDOS 7
$100 + 6 = 106; (7 + 1) \times 106 = 848; 848 - 25 = 823$
$(9 \times 3) - 5 = 22; (10 \times 10) + 22 = 122; 122 \times 7 = 854$
DISPERSAL

Round 91

ODOURLESS 9, SOLDERS 7, DOSSER 6
FELONIES 8, ONESELF 7, FLEETS
EUPHORIC 8, COUGHER 7, GOPHER 6
PROSTATE 8, TAMPERS 7, TEAPOT 6
$7 \times (100 + 25) = 875; 875 + 50 = 925; 925 - 7 = 918$
$100 + 50 + 6 = 156; 156 \times 5 = 780; 780 + 4 - 1 = 783$
ALLOWANCE

Round 92

BEWILDER 8, TREBLED 7, BELTER 6
CLEARWING 9, CLEARING 8, WRANGLE 7
SUCTORIAL 9, CURTAILS 8, RITUALS 7
SHAMBOLIC 9, CHOLIAMB 8, ABOLISH 7
$(9 + 1) \times 75 = 750; 750 - (9 \times 2) = 732$
$8 \times 25 = 200; 4 + (10/10) = 5; (200 + 5) \times 3 = 615$
MORTICIAN

Round 93

BOATHOUSE 9, ATHEOUS 7, BATHOS 6
RETRACING 9, CATERING 8, GRANITE 7
SINEWING 8, SEWING 6, BINGE 5
DENOUNCE 8, UNDONE 6, CONED 5
$75 + 50 + 10 + 9 = 144; (8 \times 100) + 144 = 944$
$25 - (7 + 4) = 14; 14 \times 75 = 1050; 1050 - (9 \times 8) = 978$
BICKERING

Round 94

SHABBIEST 9, TABBIES 7, BABIES 6
SPILLAGE 8, PILLAGE 7, SILAGE 6
PROPHETIC 9, CHOPPIER 8, PITCHER 7
CLAMMIEST 9, CLIMATES 8, LACIEST 7
$(75/25) + (100/50) = 5; 5 \times 8 \times 9 = 360$
$(7 + 3) \times 10 = 100; (6 \times 100) - 8 = 592$
PHILANDER

Round 95

PROOFING 8, ROOFING 7, ROWING 6
BRASSERIE 9, BRASSIER 8, SIERRAS 7
TERMINUS 8, ROUTINE 7, TUNERS 6
CLUBHOUSE 9, BLOUSE 6, CLUES 5
$(2 \times 7) + 9 = 23; 23 \times 25 = 575; 575 + 10 = 585$
$(6 \times 2) - 1 = 11; 100 + 11 = 111; (3 + 2) \times 111 = 555$
DIFFICULT

Round 96

RETARDANT 9, NARRATED 8, TARTARE 7
CULMINATE 9, CLIMATE 7, MENTAL 6
MEGASTORE 9, GAMESTER 8, STEAMER 7
SENIORITY 9, TYROSINE 8, NOISIER 7
$75 - 4 = 71; (5 + 4) \times 71 = 639; 639 - (50/25) = 637$
$8 \times (75 - 4) = 568; (50/2) - 4 = 21; 568 - 21 = 547$
PARAGRAPH

Round 97

PNEUMATIC 9, PETUNIA 7, PEANUT 6
ALPENHORN 9, PLANNER 7, PAROLE 6
HARANGUED 9, UNHEARD 7, AGENDA 6

NIGHTWEAR 9, WATERING 8, RIGHTEN 7
$(9 + 4) \times 50 = 650; (7 \times 5) - 6 = 29; 650 + 29 = 679$
$3 \times 100 = 300; 9 \times 7 = 63; 300 - 63 = 237$
ROUGHNESS

Round 98

CRUSTACEA 9, ACCURATE 8, ACCUSER 7
EQUISETUM 9, MESQUITE 8, QUIETUS 7
BILLYCAN 8, LUNACY 6, BULLY 5
GABERDINE 9, BEARDING 8, BANDIER 7
$7 \times 6 \times 3 = 126; (126 - 8) \times 8 = 944; 944 - 3 = 941$
$2 \times 7 \times 50 = 700; 8 + 4 - 1 = 11; 700 - 11 = 689$
INCLUSION

Round 99

JAUNDICE 8, INJURED 7, DANCER 6
TEENAGER 8, EARTHEN 7, HANGER 6
ALLOCATED 9, COLLATED 8, LOCATED 7
BEZIQUE 7, PIQUET 6, QUIET 5
$(5 + 4) \times 75 = 675; 675 + 50 = 725; 725 + 4 - 3 = 726$
$(6 + 5) \times 75 = 825; 825 + (6 \times 4) = 849$
QUICKSAND

Round 100

MANIFOLD 8, DIAMOND 7, ALMOND 6
PODGIEST 8, TEDIOUS 7, DEPOTS 6
CONCEITED 9, NOTICED 7, COINED 6
ALGEBRAIC 9, REGALIA 7, GARLIC 6
$(75 + 50) \times 8 = 1000; 3 \times 25 = 75; 1000 - 75 + 2 = 927$
$75 + (100/50) = 77; 25 - (4 \times 4) = 9; 77 \times 9 = 693$
UNDOUBTED

Round 101

JINGLES 7, LOSING 6, GLOSS 5
VINEGARY 8, CRAVING 7, GRAINY 6
CRESCENDO 9, CONCEDES 8, ENDORSE 7
ORNATELY 8, PENALTY 7, TEAPOY 6
$100/4 = 25; 25 \times 25 = 625; 625 + 50 + 1 = 676$
$(5 + 4) \times (100 - 7) = 837; 837 + 6 + 6 = 849$
WITHERING

Round 102

MUTILATED 9, ALTITUDE 8, MUTATED 7
OSTEOPATH 9, POTATOES 8, TEAPOTS 7
BEHEADING 9, BIGHEAD 7, GAINED 6
PUSHOVER 8, SOUPIER 7, HOVERS 6
$(7 + 6) \times 10 = 130; (130 + 1) \times (2 \times 2) = 524$
$(9 \times 2) \times (50 - 1) = 882; 882 - 7 = 875$
PERSPIRED

Round 103

RAINBOW 7, JOINER 6, BROWN 5
PATRONIZE 9, ATROPINE 8, PAINTER 7
FALCONRY 8, CORNEAL 7, CRAYON 6
BANDAGE 7, AGENDA 6, BANJO 5
$(6 \times 3) \times 50 = 900; (5 + 1) \times 4 = 24; 900 - 24 = 876$
$5 + 3 + 1 = 9; 9 \times (75 - 1) = 666$
PURCHASED

Round 104

WEALTH 6, ALGAE 5, AXLE 4
VIOLENT 7, MOTIVE 6, LEMON 5
VANISHED 8, INVADES 7, ONSIDE 6
TUTENAG 7, NOUGAT 6, VAUNT 5
$(3 \times 6) \times (50 + 5) = 990; 990 - (9 - 7) = 988$
$8 \times 9 = 72; 72 \times (8 + 1) = 648; 648 + 2 = 650$
INTERVIEW

Round 105

OVERCOAT 8, OVERACT 7, VECTOR 6
BIZARRELY 9, LIBRARY 7, LAZIER 6
ETHMOID 7, METHOD 6, HOPED 5
PENTHOUSE 9, POTHEENS 8, ENTHUSE 7
$(3 \times 5) + 10 = 25; 25 \times 25 = 625; 625 + 6 - 7 = 624$
$(6 + 4) \times 75 = 750; 750 + 100 = 850; 850 - (3/3) = 849$
CULMINATE

Round 106

MOUSETRAP 9, TEMPURAS 8, PASTURE 7
LIMEADE 7, MENACE 6, DENIM 5
OUTLINED 8, QUOINED 7, DILUTE 6
NOMINATED 9, DOMINATE 8, DOMAINE 7
$(8 \times 5) = 40; 40 \times (7 + 1) = 320; 320 + 9 = 329$
$(4 \times 25) - 7 = 93; 93 \times (4 + 1) = 465$
TURNTABLE

Round 107

LOUSIEST 8, SOLUTES 7, TISSUE 6
FRIGATE 7, BOATER 6, BRIEF 5
AQUIFER 7, FIGURE 6, QUIRE 5
BOOGIES 7, IMPOSE 6, POISE 5
$(7 + 2) \times 50 = 450; 450 + 8 = 458; 458 \times (5 - 3) = 916$
$3 \times 75 = 225; 225 - 5 - 4 - 1 = 215; 215 \times 4 = 860$
TRIBUTARY

Round 108

EXAMPLE 7, FEMALE 6, EXPEL 5
CONSOLER 8, COLOGNE 7, LONGER 6
GRIMACED 8, RAGTIME 7, MIDGET 6
OPUNTIAS 8, OUTSPAN 7, PATIOS 6
$8 \times 2 \times 2 = 32; 32 \times 25 = 800; 800 - (10 + 9) = 781$
$4 \times 3 \times 3 = 36; (36 + 1) \times 25 = 925; 925 - 2 = 923$
NUMBERING

Round 109

PROGRADE 8, VAPORED 7, GROPED 6
SEDATION 8, INSTEAD 7, FASTEN 6
DILEMMAS 8, MISLEAD 7, SLIDES 6
CASCADED 8, SACCADE 7, CASHED 6
$100 - (8 + 4) = 88; 88 \times 6 = 528; 528 - (1 + 1) = 526$
$(9 + 2) \times (5 - 2) = 33; 75 + 33 = 108; 108 \times 8 = 864$
BATTERING

Round 110

TUTORAGE 8, GAROTTE 7, PUTTER 6
VANISHED 8, INVADES 7, SIENNA 6
MANICURE 8, NUMERIC 7, CRAVEN 6

434

RHEOSTAT 8, SHATTER 7, HORNET 6
$(7 + 5) \times (6 + 1) = 84; (84 \times 10) + 2 = 842$
$(9 + 2) \times 9 = 99; 99 \times 6 = 594; 594 - 8 = 586$
SPAGHETTI

Round 111

NOVELTY 7, YEOMAN 6, OVATE 5
LOZENGES 8, ENCLOSE 7, CLONES 6
GATEAUX 7, KARATE 6, GRATE 5
OTHERWISE 9, THEORISE 8, WITHERS 7
$(8 - 6) \times 75 = 150; 150 + 5 + 4 = 159; 159 \times 5 = 795$
$100 + 10 + 7 = 117; (8/2) \times 117 = 468$
INSINCERE

Round 112

HERNIATE 8, HAIRNET 7, RETINA 6
ALCOVES 7, COAXES 6, SLAVE 5
PILOTED 7, POLICE 6, OPTIC 5
AMNIOTIC 8, ACONITE 7, INMATE 6
$(6 \times 25) + 50 = 200; (200 + 6) \times 4 = 824; 824 - 4 = 820$
$(6 \times 25) + 3 = 153; 153 \times 2 = 306; 306 + 5 = 311$
ENDORSING

Round 113

PENTODES 8, POINTED 7, STONED 6
CORONAL 7, RACOON 6, CORAL 5
READMITS 8, WARTIME 7, MISTER 6
FETCHES 7, THEMES 6, COMET 5
$(6 + 3) \times (100 - 10) = 810; 810 - (7 - 2) = 805$
$9 \times 9 \times 3 \times 3 = 729$
QUIESCENT

Round 114

TINKLED 7, PINKED 6, UNLIT 5
FRIVOLED 8, DIVORCE 7, FOLDER 6
SHEEPDOG 8, HOOPED 6, HOODS 5
HABITAT 7, BATTER 6, HEART 5
$(9 \times 10) - 10 = 80; (80 + 1) \times 9 = 729; 729 - 100 = 629$
$6 + (100/25) = 10; 75 + 9 = 84; 84 \times 10 = 840$
LIMITLESS

Round 115

LOUNGED 7, TONGUE 6, TOLLED 6
CHARMER 7, MARROW 6, CHORE 5
STOPGAP 7, POTASH 6, HOIST 5
ESSAYING 8, SAYINGS 7, VEGANS 6
$(8 \times 3) + 1 = 25; 25 \times 25 = 625; 625 - (4 - 1) = 622$
$100 + 75 + 50 = 225; 225 \times 3 = 675; 675 - (4 \times 4) = 659$
RADIATION

Round 116

DOUBTER 7, DITHER 6, THIRD 5
PILLAGE 7, GOALIE 6, LOYAL 5
ENDOCARPS 9, OPERANDS 8, RESPOND 7
TIDEWAYS 8, WIDGETS 7, SWEATY 6
$8 \times (75 - 6) = 552; 2 + (4/4) = 3; 552 + 3 = 555$
$(8 + 2) \times 7 = 70; 70 \times 5 = 350; 350 - 7 = 343$
TOUGHENED

435

Round 117

PATHOGEN 8, HEXAGON 7, POTAGE 6
FORGIVEN 8, VERTIGO 7, ROVING 6
ELOQUENT 8, OPULENT 7, TOUPEE 6
DISMANTLE 9, MANLIEST 8, STAINED 7
$(9 \times 7) - 5 = 58$; $58 \times 6 = 348$; $348 - 100 = 248$
$10 \times (10 + 4) = 140$; $140 + 6 + 2 = 148$; $148 \times 5 = 740$
SATELLITE

Round 118

UPRATE 6, AVERT 5, FARE 4
TETANUS 7, FASTEN 6, TUNES 5
SEETHING 8, SHOEING 7, INGEST 6
MINIVERS 8, VERMIN 6, VIRUS 5
$(9 + 8) \times (50 - 4) = 782$; $782 + 5 - 3 = 784$
$2 \times 7 \times 50 = 700$; $(4 \times 8) - 25 = 7$; $700 - 7 = 693$
WEALTHIER

Round 119

ADMIXES 7, SHAMED 6, WAXES 5
MOONLET 7, TOWNEE 6, MELON 5
FLUIDRAM 8, MAUDLIN 7, MARLIN 6
CEREALS 7, CALLER 6, LARGE 5
$8 \times 6 = 48$; $48 - (5 - 1) = 44$; $44 \times 7 = 308$
$(4 \times 25) - (5 + 2) = 93$; $3 \times 3 = 9$; $93 \times 9 = 837$
RECOUPING

Round 120

UPENDING 8, PENGUIN 7, GUNNED 6
VITRIOL 7, FILTER 6, OLIVE 5
AEROSOL 7, SOLACE 6, GEARS 5
MISRATED 8, SIDEARM 7, MUSTER 6
$7 + 7 - 3 = 11$; $50 + 11 = 61$; $61 \times 4 = 264$
$(2 \times 9) + 7 = 25$; $(4 + 1) \times 6 = 30$; $25 \times 30 = 750$
TRANSCEND

Round 121

URETHRAL 8, BLATHER 7, HERBAL 6
FOOTMARKS 9, FORMATS 7, MOTORS 6
MORGUES 7, SOURED 6, DRUMS 5
APOLUNES 8, CAPSULE 7, PLACES 6
$(6 \times 25) - 3 = 147$; $(5 + 1) \times 147 = 882$
$3 \times (75 - 1) = 222$; $50 - 8 = 42$; $222 + 42 = 264$
WHIRLPOOL

Round 122

TERRIFY 7, FILTER 6, RIFLE 5
BROACHES 8, CARBOYS 7, CHORES 6
HEXAPOD 7, HOAXED 6, APHID 5
YOUNGER 7, GRUNGE 6, PRONE 5
$6 \times (9 + 1) = 60$; $60 - 2 = 58$; $58 \times (5 \times 2) = 580$
$(3 \times 8) + 5 + 2 = 31$; $31 \times 25 = 775$; $775 + 2 = 777$
TANTALISE

Round 123

MOISTER 7, JOSTLE 6, MERIT 5
COGNATES 8, NOSEBAG 7, AGENTS 6
SITUATE 7, STATUE 6, FUMES 5

VINEGAR 7, VAGINA 6, GRAVE 5
$(10 + 9) \times 50 = 950; \ 950 - (6 \times 6) = 914$
$(8 \times 100) + (3 \times 7) = 821; \ 821 - (50/25) = 819$
GROTESQUE

Round 124

FIREDAMP 8, DEMIREP 7, FAIRED 6
DOORMATS 8, STARDOM 7, SMOOTH 6
EXORCISTS 9, COEXISTS 8, COSIEST 7
DOCKAGE 7, TACKED 6, KITED 5
$75 - (9/9) = 74; \ 5 + (10/10) = 6; \ 74 \times 6 = 444$
$(8 - 6) + 1 = 3; \ 3 \times 7 \times 25 = 525; \ 525 + 8 = 533$
BEDSPREAD

Round 125

TZIGANE 7, NEGATE 6, TINGE 5
POOREST 7, TOWERS 6, WROTE 5
FRAILTY 7, RATIFY 6, TARDY 5
QUEERLY 7, PURELY 6, EQUIP 5
$25 - 3 - 2 = 20; \ 4 \times 20 = 80; \ (7 \times 100) - 80 = 620$
$(8 \times 8) - 6 = 58; \ 58 + 75 = 133 \times 7 = 931$
FORSAKING

Round 126

OVERLAND 8, REMOVAL 7, RANDOM 6
INSPIRER 8, SPINIER 7, SNIPER 6
CESTODE 7, STODGE 6, BEGET 5
BARONET 7, ORANGE 6, BORNE 5
$(3 \times 50) + 10 = 160; \ 160 \times 4 = 640; \ 640 + 2 = 642$
$(7 \times 8) + 5 = 61; \ 61 \times 4 = 244; \ 244 + 9 = 253$
INCORRECT

Round 127

JITTERED 8, ERUDITE 7, JETTED 6
PREDATION 9, ORDINATE 8, PAROTID 7
FISHMEAL 8, HIMSELF 7, FLAMES 6
FRUCTOSE 8, FORGETS 7, FOSTER 6
$(5 \times 75) + 100 = 475; \ (2 \times 6) - 1 = 11; \ 475 - 11 = 464$
$10 \times (7 + 4) = 110; \ (110 - 1) \times 8 = 872; \ 872 + 3 = 875$
EVOLUTION

Round 128

LANGUISH 8, SEALING 7, SINGLE 6
SALLOWED 8, SWOLLEN 7, WALLED 6
ENGRAVED 8, ANGERED 7, GARDEN 6
GREYHOUND 9, HYDROGEN 8, YOUNGER 7
$6 \times (75 + 6) = 486; \ 486 - 100 = 386$
$75 + 8 + 3 = 86; \ 86 \times 8 = 688; \ 688 + 6 + 3 = 697$
LUBRICATE

Round 129

ORDAINER 8, RANDIER 7, ROARED 6
MARINERS 8, SEMINAR 7, INSURE 6
ELECTRUM 8, LECTURE 7, CUTLER 6
NOTABLE 7, COATED 6, BLADE 5
$100 - (7 + 6) = 87; \ 87 \times (5 + 5) = 870; \ 870 - 2 = 868$
$(4 + 1) \times 50 = 250; \ 250 + 9 + 8 + 7 = 274$
UPSETTING

Round 130

ANECDOTE 8, CLEANED 7, DECANT 6
SLOGGER 7, UGLIER 6, ROGUE 5
SNAKIER 7, SIENNA 6, INNER 5
JUKEBOX 7, JOUKED 6, BIJOU 5
$7 \times 3 \times 25 = 525; 525 - (10/5) = 523$
$9 \times 9 \times 10 = 810; 25 - (2 \times 7) = 11; 810 + 11 = 821$
PROSECUTE

Round 131

VOLTAGE 7, OCTAVE 6, COVET 5
DILUTION 8, UNTOLD 6, LIMIT 5
PRISONED 8, SOUPIER 7, POURED 6
SUAVEST 7, STAVES 6, PASTE 5
$(2 \times 50) - 6 = 94; 94 \times 4 = 376; 376 + 4 - 3 = 377$
$75 + (7 - 3) = 79; (6 + 6) \times 79 = 948$
ACCORDION

Round 132

POLECAT 7, OCTAVE 6, CLOVE 5
JETTISONS 9, STONIEST 8, NOSIEST 7
EXPENDS 7, SPONGE 6, DOPES 5
ARMISTICE 9, SCIMITAR 8, AIRTIME 7
$100 + 75 + 50 + 25 = 250; 250 - 3 = 247; 247 \times 3 = 741$
$(9 + 7) \times 9 = 144$
DIFFERING

Round 133

IGNORED 7, INDIGO 6, IRONY 5
DIAGNOSED 9, ADENOIDS 8, AGONIES 7
ROULADE 7, VALOUR 6, DROVE 5
UNDERUSED 9, SUNDERED 8, ENDURED 7
$(4 \times 10) - 3 = 37; 37 \times 25 = 925; 925 + 7 + 5 = 937$
$9 \times (100 - 9) = 819; 6 + (2/2) = 7; 819 + 7 = 826$
EXPOUNDED

Round 134

WOOLLIES 8, SWILLED 7, SLOWED 6
OVULATE 7, VOLANT 6, NAVAL 5
GREYISH 7, RUSHED 6, HIDES 5
PROFANELY 9, FOREPLAY 8, PALFREY 7
$(7 \times 25) + 7 = 182; 182 \times 5 = 910; 910 + (8/2) = 914$
$(8 \times 75) + 25 = 625; 625 - (6/3) = 623$
AUTOGRAPH

Round 135

REPLIES 7, EERILY 6, PRIZE 5
NOURISH 7, ONRUSH 6, SHORN 5
PLECTRUM 8, CRUMPET 7, TRIPLE 6
DISCOED 7, ESCUDO 6, DICED 5
$(9 - 4) \times (100 + 2) = 510; 510 + 75 = 585; 585 - 7 = 578$
$6 - (1 + 1) = 4; 4 \times (50 + 8) = 232; 232 + 7 = 239$
PROTESTED

Round 136

ALRIGHT 7, SAILOR 6, LIGHT 5
DISASTER 8, TIGRESS 7, STAIRS 6
PAIRING 7, INWARD 6, WRING 5

438

ESCALATED 9, ESCALADE 8, DELATES 7
100 − (2 × 10) = 80; 6 × 80 = 480; 480 − 9 = 471
(75/25) × 100 = 300; 300 + 50 + 2 = 352; 352 × 2 = 704
SUFFOCATE

Round 137

DENOTED 7, HUNTED 6, ENDED 5
FLOURISH 8, OURSELF 7, RELISH 6
FACILELY 8, IDEALLY 7, FILLED 6
DIVIDER 7, DIVERT 6, TIRED 5
100 − (10/5) = 98; 98 × 7 = 686; 686 − 50 + 3 = 639
7 × (4 + 3) = 49; 49 × 6 = 294
CONSONANT

Round 138

VAPIDLY 7, DEPLOY 6, YIELD 5
FIXATED 7, FIESTA 6, TAXES 5
THUMPED 7, TEDIUM 6, THYME 5
ICEBOAT 7, COATED 6, DEBIT 5
(25 + 2) × 10 = 270; (270 + 4) × 2 = 548; 548 + 7 = 555
9 × 8 = 72; 10 − 2 = 8; (72 + 1) × 8 = 584
SMOOTHING

Round 139

ARGALIS 7, SPIRAL 6, SPRIG 5
CROAKILY 8, SCARILY 7, CLOAKS 6
RELATOR 7, ZEALOT 6, ALTER 5
UGLIER 6, GRUEL 5, RELY 4
10 × (9 + 8) = 170; 170 + 75 = 245; 245 − (9 − 8) = 244
2 × (50 + 1) = 102; 102 + 75 + 9 = 186
DEHYDRATE

Round 140

OBTRUSIVE 9, VITREOUS 8, BUSTIER 7
BLUSHER 7, HERBAL 6, RELAX 5
POACHED 7, COATED 6, PHAGE 5
DALLIANCE 9, ALLIANCE 8, CEDILLA 7
4 × (10 − 1) = 36; (36 − 1) × 25 = 875
(10 + 8) × 50 = 900; (5 × 8) − 7 = 33; 900 + 33 = 933
CONGEALED

Round 141

YOURSELF 8, OURSELF 7, SURELY 6
VICEROY 7, DRIVEL 6, COVER 5
CARTONED 8, REDCOAT 7, TRACED 6
CAGOULES 8, GLUCOSE 7, SOLACE 6
9 + 6 = 15; 25 − 2 = 23; 15 × 23 = 345; 345 + 1 + 1 = 347
8 × (50 − 9) = 328; 328 − 10 − 7 = 311
PLOUGHMAN

Round 142

SABOTEUR 8, BOATERS 7, BEAUTY 6
GRANULES 8, WRANGLE 7, LAGERS 6
BASSIST 7, BOASTS 6, AUTOS 5
BOARDING 8, ADORING 7, DRAGON 6
(4 × 7) + 4 = 32; 32 × 25 = 800; 800 + 10 + 2 = 812
4 × (100 + 50) = 600; 9 − (75/25) = 6; 600 + 6 = 606
SOMETHING

Round 143

JUNKIES 7, INJURE 6, VIRUS 5
UNGLAZED 8, DANGLES 7, SLUDGE 6
BAYONET 7, GOATEE 6, AGENT 5
LIBERATE 8, BLOATER 7, REBATE 6
$(10 + 7) \times 50 = 850; (2 \times 6) + 9 = 21; 850 + 21 = 871$
$100 - 7 = 93; 93 \times 2 \times 2 = 372$
ABSCONDED

Round 144

THINNED 7, ENGINE 6, THING 5
IMPLODES 8, MILDEST 7, POSTED 6
ASTOUND 7, DIVOTS 6, VAUNT 5
PLACATE 7, PACKER 6, CREAK 5
$(2 \times 3) + 1 = 7; 7 \times 6 \times 5 \times 4 = 840$
$3 \times (2 + 1) = 9; 9 \times 4 \times 3 = 108; 108 \times 8 = 864$
MATERNITY

Round 145

GADFLIES 8, LADIES 6, FIELD 5
BOASTERS 8, BASKETS 7, SORBET 6
TETRAPOD 8, ROTATED 7, POTTER 6
BIPLANES 8, LESBIAN 7, SALINE 6
$(7 - 1) \times 100 = 600; 9 \times (4 + 1) = 45; 600 - 45 = 555$
$10 \times (9 + 7) = 160; 8 \times 7 = 56; 160 + 56 = 216; 216 + 10 = 226$
POLLUTING

Round 146

ARMIGER 7, RETAIL 6, GRIME 5
RANNIES 8, SPANNER 7, CRANES 6
LOATHING 8, SALTING 7, GLOATS 6
MONETARY 8, ANYMORE 7, ORNATE 6
$5 \times (4 + 1) = 25; 25 \times 25 = 625; 625 + 10 - 7 = 628$
$8 + 6 + 3 = 17; 50 + 1 = 51; 17 \times 51 = 867$
SPECIALTY

Round 147

FRUITAGE 8, OUTRAGE 7, FIGURE 6
CATEGORY 8, CORDAGE 7, GRACED 6
FOLKISH 7, GHOULS 6, FLOGS 5
INTERFACE 9, FRENETIC 8, FIANCEE 7
$75 + 25 + 8 - 3 = 105; 105 \times 9 = 945$
$(100 + 75) \times 5 = 875 + 10 = 885$
IRRITATED

Round 148

MINERAL 7, WAILED 6, DREAM 5
SMARTIES 8, FIRMEST 7, FIESTA 6
NOTIFYING 9, TOYING 6, INGOT 5
BRIEFEST 8, FORTIES 7, FIBRES 6
$9 \times 50 = 450; 450 + 25 - 3 = 472; 472 \times 2 = 944$
$50 + 7 - 6 = 51; 8 + 8 + 1 = 17; 17 \times 51 = 867$
COMFORTED

Round 149

DURATIVE 8, VIRTUAL 7, VALUED 6
GOLFERS 7, SLEIGH 6, RIFLE 5
GLEAMING 8, NIGGLES 7, SILAGE 6

DENSITY 7, NUDITY 6, VINES 5
$(5 + 3) \times 75 = 600; 9 \times (7 - 4) = 27; 600 - 27 = 573$
$9 - (50/25) = 7; 100 - (6/6) = 99; 7 \times 99 = 693$
DORMITORY

Round 150

OPUNTIA 7, KIDNAP 6, POINT 5
SIMILAR 7, GARISH 6, RAILS 5
UNSIZED 7, UNISEX 6, SEDAN 50
PADOUKS 7, SOAKED 6, SPOKE 5
$50 - 3 = 47; 10 + 10 + 5 - 4 = 21; 47 \times 21 = 987$
$(2 \times 5) + 3 = 13; 75 + 13 = 88; 88 \times 8 = 704$
ELEGANTLY

Round 151

AMMONIA 7, ANIMAL 6, MANIA 5
CANOEIST 8, JACONET 7, ACTION 6
SALIENCY 8, ANGELIC 7, NICELY 6
ATTEND 6, NAKED 5, DATA 4
$8 \times (100 - 10) = 720; 720 - 3 - 1 = 716$
$(2 \times 9) + 1 = 19; 19 \times 25 = 475; 475 - (10 + 3) = 462$
APPEARING

Round 152

DIALOGUE 8, PLAGUED 7, LAPDOG 6
HEADLINE 8, INHALED 7, WAILED 6
NATIVELY 8, VIOLENT 7, LITANY 6
ERUPTION 8, JUNIPER 7, PUNTER 6
$75 + 8 - 5 = 78; (78 \times 10) - 1 = 779$
$6 \times 5 \times 2 \times 2 = 120; 120 - 7 = 113; 113 \times 8 = 904$
WEAKENING

Round 153

NUTCASE 7, JAUNTS 6, SCANT 5
BEGONIA 7, OBTAIN 6, JINGO 5
RENEWING 8, WARNING 7, REGAIN 6
TARGETED 8, AVERTED 7, VETTED 6
$9 \times 7 = 63; 63 \times (10 - 2) = 504; 504 - 100 = 404$
$50 - 1 = 49; (3 \times 5) - 1 = 14; 49 \times 14 = 686$
PROTRUDED

Round 154

NIGHTWEAR 9, WATERING 8, HAIRNET 7
ARGUFY 6, RUGBY 5, BEAU 4
INFRARED 8, RANDIER 7, FRIEND 6
DISPUTES 8, STUMPED 7, UPSETS 6
$(6 \times 6) - 2 = 34; 25 - 2 = 23; 34 \times 23 = 782; 782 + 3 = 785$
$(75 - 1) \times 2 = 148; 148 \times 2 = 296; 296 - 6 = 290$
FOREFRONT

Round 155

TEACHABLE 9, HEATABLE 8, ACTABLE 7
POACHES 7, PSYCHO 6, SPACE 5
LETTERED 8, RELATED 7, DEALER 6
ECHOGRAM 8, MONARCH 7, CHROME 6
$50 + 9 - 8 = 51; 51 \times 7 = 357; 357 - (10/10) = 356$
$8 \times (9 + 2) = 88; 9 \times (88 - 5) = 747; 747 + 1 = 748$
DEVOURING

Round 156

COULISSE 8, VISCOSE 7, SLUICE 6
INDOORS 7, DISOWN 6, DROWN 5
GRAVITON 8, ADORING 7, VIRAGO 6
FAILURE 7, PURIFY 6, FLARE 5
$7 + 5 - 1 = 11; 3 \times 11 = 33; 9 \times 75 = 675; 675 - 33 = 642$
$2 \times (4 + 1) = 10; 10 \times (100 - 4) = 960$
IMBALANCE

Round 157

BOREHOLE 8, BELCHER 7, BREECH 6
PIERCER 7, CREEPY 6, PRICE 5
FOOTAGE 7, GOOFED 6, ADOPT 5
MATADOR 7, DREAMT 6, AVERT 5
$6 \times 50 = 300; 25 \times 3 = 75; 300 - (75/75) = 299$
$(9 + 4) \times 25 = 325; 325 + 6 + 2 = 333$
FLUCTUATE

Round 158

ROAMING 7, LOWING 6, GROAN 5
UPGRADE 7, LAAGER 6, PURGE 5
DISTANCE 8, CHAINED 7, HINTED 6
BROODIEST 9, STEROID 7, BOOTED 6
$10 \times (5 + 5) = 100; (100 + 7) \times (6 + 3) = 963$
$100 - 3 = 97; (8 + 2) \times 97 = 970; 970 - 4 = 966$
STIPULATE

Round 159

DRAWBACK 8, WRACKED 7, ARCADE 6
LOWLIEST 8, TOILERS 7, WRITES 6
SCRAPPED 8, SIDECAR 7, ASPIRE 6
ONESELF 7, LOWEST 6, FLEET 5
$(75 + 3) \times (5 + 4) = 702; 702 + 2 = 704$
$3 \times (3 + 4) = 21; 21 \times 25 = 525; 525 + 8 - 6 = 527$
ADDICTION

Round 160

SQUARELY 8, EQUABLY 7, BARLEY 6
HOLIDAYS 8, HASTILY 7, STOLID 6
DEFLATE 7, FAILED 6, HATED 5
DOGFISH 7, OXHIDE 6, HOSED 5
$25 + 6 - 1 = 30; 9 + 7 = 16; 30 \times 16 = 480; 480 - 2 = 478$
$(9 \times 25) + 6 + 3 = 234; 234 \times 4 = 936; 936 + 2 = 938$
CONCEALED

Round 161

DEROGATED 9, DEGRADE 7, GOATEE 6
TROPICAL 8, PARBOIL 7, COITAL 6
ORBITAL 7, ARTFUL 6, ULTRA 5
TAPESTRY 8, TEAPOTS 7, SPORTY 6
$50 + (9 \times 4) = 86; 86 \times 7 = 602$
$10 + 1 - 4 = 7; (100 + 6) \times 7 = 742; 742 + 5 = 747$
PRIVILEGE

Round 162

FIREDAMP 8, PYRAMID 7, DREAMY 6
FINALIZED 9, INFIDEL 7, FINALE 6
VIOLATED 8, TABLOID 7, BOLTED 6

PURGATORY 9, PORTRAY 7, YOGURT 6
6 + 5 + 4 = 15; 15 × 25 = 375; 375 + 8 = 383
7 × 7 × 3 = 147; 147 + (5/5) = 148; 148 × 3 = 444
RENDITION

Round 163

MIAOWED 7, MILDEW 6, GLEAM 5
THORAXES 8, EARSHOT 7, HOAXES 6
TOASTED 7, SEADOG 6, GOATS 5
ANCESTRY 8, CRYSTAL 7, TRACES 6
(10 + 9) × 4 = 76; 76 × (5 × 2) = 760
7 × (75 + 25) = 700; 50 − (9 + 6) = 35; 700 − 35 = 665
DASTARDLY

Round 164

DRIFTER 7, FIDGET 6, FRUIT 5
CHAPERON 8, ANOTHER 7, TRANCE 6
OBLIVION 8, OLIVINE 7, VIOLIN 6
EPIBLAST 8, POTABLE 7, ALBEIT 6
75 + 5 = 80; 80 × (8 + 4) = 960; 960 − 9 = 951
100 − (7 × 4) = 72; 72 × 8 = 576; 576 − 2 = 574
GAMBOLLED

Round 165

STUPEFY 7, PUTZES 6, PIETY 5
BROADEST 8, BOASTED 7, MASTER 6
PALACES 7, CANOES 6, PLACE 5
LACKEYED 8, TACKLED 7, TACKED 6
5 × (25 + 3) = 140; 140 × 7 = 980
(5 × 5) + 10 = 35; 35 × 25 = 875; 875 − (10 + 1) = 864
CIVILISED

Round 166

DILEMMAS 8, MISLEAD 7, MEDIUM 6
OVERCAST 8, AVOCETS 7, CARROT 6
MIGRATES 8, MASTERY 7, ARMIES 6
INTERPLAY 9, TRIPLANE 8, PAINTER 7
5 × 6 × 3 × 3 = 270; 270 + 4/4 = 271
(6 − 2) × (75 + 10) = 340; 340 + 7 = 347
FRUMPIEST

Round 167

SURVEYOR 8, DEVOURS 7, DROVER 6
JAWBONES 8, BANJOES 7, ABSENT 6
CHARIOTS 8, HARICOT 7, CHARTS 6
SUBLATED 8, BUSTLED 7, WASTED 6
(6 × 75) − (7 × 5) = 415; 415 + (50/25) = 417
(3 × 5) + 1 = 16; 16 × 50 = 800; 800 + 4 − 3 = 801
HORSEBACK

Round 168

ROWBOAT 7, BOOTER 6, ORATE 5
CURABLE 7, WARBLE 6, CRAWL 5
MIDWIFE 7, DIMWIT 6, MEDIA 5
SCENERY 7, WINERY 6, CREWS 5
7 − (8 − 7) = 6; (6 × 100) − 4 = 596
(10 × 25) − 2 = 248; 9 − 5 = 4; 248 × 4 = 992
BREAKFAST

Round 169

FIREBUGS 8, FIGURES 7, BIGGER 6
INSULTED 8, DUSTBIN 7, BLINDS 6
WISHBONE 8, TOWNIES 7, BESTOW 6
EXOTERIC 8, COTERIE 7, EXCITE 6
$(6 + 4) \times 50 = 500$; $500 - (9 + 8) = 483$
$(50 + 8) \times (8 + 5) = 754$; $754 + (3 - 1) = 756$
OTHERWISE

Round 170

NAIVELY 7, MENIAL 6, ANVIL 5
EPIDURAL 8, PREVAIL 7, REPAID 6
MOONFISH 8, NOISOME 7, MONIES 6
HOTLINE 7, BOTHIE 6, THINE 5
$3 \times (75/25) = 9$; $9 \times 50 = 450$; $450 + 100 + 4 = 554$
$(7 - 1) \times 6 = 36$; $36 \times 8 = 288$
JOURNEYED

Round 171

CONSUME 7, POUNCE 6, SCONE 5
FLYWEIGHT 9, WHITEFLY 8, WEIGHTY 7
ROUNDELS 8, SOUNDLY 7, YONDER 6
KEYBOARD 8, BROADEN 7, BRANDY 6
$(8 \times 100) - 75 = 725$; $725 - 6 = 719$
$3 \times (2 + 1) = 9$; $100 + 2 + 1 = 103$; $9 \times 103 = 927$
BRIEFCASE

Round 172

WALTZED 7, ZEALOT 6, DELTA 5
POWERFUL 8, FLOURED 7, POURED 6
REARMOST 8, STAMPER 7, POSTER 6
MAYPOLE 7, EPONYM 6, FLAME 5
$9 + 5 = 14$; $25 + 8 = 33$; $14 \times 33 = 462$; $462 + 7 = 469$
$50 + (75/25) = 53$; $8 + 2 = 10$; $53 \times 10 = 530$
MEDITATED

Round 173

FRIVOLED 8, FORGIVE 7, LODGER 6
GUARANTY 8, UNITARY 7, GRAINY 6
GUILDERS 8, GROUSED 7, SOURED 6
REMOVAL 7, MOTHER 6, LOVER 5
$100 - 5 = 95$; $(7 + 3) \times 95 = 950$; $950 - 4 = 946$
$100 + 75 - 2 = 173$; $173 \times 4 = 692$
MATCHLESS

Round 174

RAMEKIN 7, REMAIN 6, HIKER 5
CAPITOLS 8, OPTICAL 7, POLICY 6
OXYGENATE 9, GOATEE 6, TANGO 5
CENTAVOS 8, OCTAVES 7, ENCASE 6
$(10 + 8) \times 50 = 900$; $100/4 = 25$; $900 + 25 = 925$
$(3 \times 25) - 1 = 74$; $74 \times 9 = 666$
AEROPLANE

Round 175

CRUDELY 7, CLOVER 6, CLOUD 5
MANIFESTO 9, AMNIOTES 8, MOISTEN 7
GLEAMING 8, NIGGLES 7, MANGLE 6

HOCUSING 8, ANGUISH 7, CHAINS 6
5 × (100 + 50) = 750; 4 + 2 = 6; 6/6 = 1; 750 − 1 = 749
6 × (25 − 2) = 138; 138 − 4 = 134; 134 × 5 = 670; 670 − 1 = 669
PROCESSOR

Round 176

HUSBANDER 9, UNSHARED 8, BRUSHED 7
OBEYING 7, IGNORE 6, BEING 5
NUCELLAR 8, NUCLEAR 7, RECALL 6
CARIBOUS 8, CARIOUS 7, SOCIAL 6
(10 − 8) × 100 = 200; (8 × 7) − 10 = 46; 200 + 46 = 246
7 + 2 + 2 = 11; 11 + (4 × 25) = 111; 111 × 8 = 888
CATHEDRAL

Round 177

ADHESIVE 8, HEAVIES 7, DEVISE 6
TELEMARK 8, ETERNAL 7, MARKET 6
AMYLOID 7, CYMBAL 6, MADLY 5
FOUNTAIN 8, TONNEAU 7, INFANT 6
(9 + 8) × 25 = 425; 425 − 6 = 419; 419 × (1 + 1) = 838
(8 × 25) + 6 = 206; 206 × 4 = 824
SPARKLING

Round 178

RANDOMIZE 9, ROMANIZE 8, ANEROID 7
FROGMEN 7, WOOFER 6, FROWN 5
LOWERING 8, COWGIRL 7, WINGER 6
BAYONET 7, BANNER 6, ABORT 5
75 + 4 + 1 = 80; 80 × 9 = 720
(3 × 3) × (50 + 25) = 675; 675 − (6 + 2) = 667
LEATHERED

Round 179

MACKEREL 8, FRECKLE 7, REMAKE 6
TAURINE 7, TANNER 6, ANNEX 5
ORGANDIE 8, READING 7, FRINGE 6
VISCID 6, DISCS 5, VIED 4
3 × 2 × 25 = 150; 150 − (4 + 4) = 142; 142 × 6 = 852
7 × 5 = 35; 35 × 25 = 875; 875 + 9 + 3 = 887
PROVOKING

Round 180

FASHIONED 9, ADHESION 8, ANODISE 7
RESIDENCE 9, SCREENED 8, SINCERE 7
SECRETIVE 9, EVICTEES 8, SERVICE 7
DIMETRIC 8, TIMIDER 7, CHIMED 6
2 × 3 × 5 = 30; (30 + 1) × 25 = 775; 775 + 7 = 782
(100 + 2) × 9 = 918; 918 − 75 = 843; 843 + 4 − 3 = 844
HONOURING

Round 181

AIRMAILED 9, ALARMED 7, RADIAL 6
EMPLOYED 8, POLYMER 7, ELOPED 6
DEBRIEFS 8, SEABIRD 7, BRIDES 6
REPAIRED 8, PARRIED 7, HARPED 6
(6 + 4) × 75 = 750; 8 + (5 − 3) = 10; 750 + 10 = 760
8 × (10 + 5) = 120; 120 × 7 = 840; 840 + 1 = 841
HARVESTED

Round 182

PROMOTED 8, TORPEDO 7, ROOTED 6
POLKAING 8, PARKING 7, ROPING 6
KISSOGRAM 9, ORGASMS 7, SMIRKS 6
SCREAMED 8, SECURED 7, DREAMS 6
$(100 - 25) \times 8 = 600$; $(7 \times 4) + 1 = 29$; $600 + 29 = 629$
$(50/5) + 3 = 13$; $13 \times 25 = 325$; $325 - 8 = 317$
IMPLICATE

Round 183

PULSATED 8, DEFAULT 7, LAPSED 6
OBTRUSIVE 9, VITREOUS 8, BUSTIER 7
AFTERCARE 9, TERRACE 7, FERRET 6
JALAPENO 8, WEAPON 6, ALONE 5
$(50/5) \times 75 = 750$; $750 + 25 + 1 = 776$
$75 + 50 + 4 = 129$; $129 \times (4 + 2) = 774$; $774 + 2 = 776$
PANORAMIC

Round 184

SCRAPING 8, RASPING 7, PRANGS 6
REGIONAL 8, RAILING 7, LINGER 6
BLUEGRASS 9, GARBLES 7, ABUSES 6
DYSLEXIC 8, SEXILY 6, DISCO 5
$(4 + 3) \times 75 = 525$; $525 + 10 + (6/2) = 538$
$7 + 7 + 2 = 16$; $16 \times 50 = 800$; $800 + (5 \times 4) = 820$
INTIMATED

Round 185

POULTICE 8, COMPUTE 7, POETIC 6
QUAVERING 9, VINEGAR 7, QUIVER 6
LAPSTONE 8, POLENTA 7, PLANET 6
GUITARIST 9, GUITARS 7, ARTIST 6
$100 - 8 = 92$; $(75/25) \times 92 = 276$; $276 - 10 = 266$
$9 \times 9 = 81$; $81 \times 8 = 648$; $648 - 5 = 643$
ELONGATED

Round 186

BUREAUX 7, BUREAU 6, BUYER 5
PURCHASE 8, ACCUSER 7, PUSHER 6
REFUTABLE 9, FEATURE 7, BEATER 6
KEEPABLE 8, BLEAKER 7, BEAKER 6
$8 \times 9 \times 10 = 720$; $(3 + 4) \times 2 = 14$; $720 + 14 = 734$
$25 - (8 + 7) = 10$; $10 \times (50 + 5) = 550$; $550 - 7 = 543$
SENSATION

Round 187

SCIMITAR 8, SATIRIC 7, RACISM 6
REFINANCE 9, FIANCEE 7, REFACE 6
AEROBATIC 9, BACTERIA 8, AIRBOAT 7
DOGMATIC 8, AGOUTI 6, ADMIT 5
$(10 + 1) \times 75 = 825$; $4 \times 4 = 16$; $825 + 16 = 841$
$(9 + 5) \times 8 = 112$; $112 + 2 = 114$; $114 \times (9 - 4) = 570$
PRAGMATIC

Round 188

HANDSOME 8, DAEMONS 7, DOMAIN 6
SCHOONER 8, CHOOSER 7, HERONS 6
UNDERHAND 9, UNHANDED 8, HUNDRED 7
ADORNMENT 9, ORNAMENT 8, MORDENT 7
$3 \times (3 + 6) = 27$; $27 \times 25 = 675$; $675 - 8 = 667$

$75 + 10 + 10 + 9 = 104; 104 \times (100/25) = 416$
SOLILOQUY

Round 189

DEERSKIN 8, KINDEST 7, TINKER 6
JACONET 7, DEACON 6, CANOE 5
ENDURABLE 9, LAUNDER 7, BURNED 6
CAHOOTS 7, STARCH 6, TORSO 5
$(3 \times 3) + 2 = 11; (75 + 1) \times 11 = 836; 836 + 100 = 936$
$5 \times 75 = 375; (50/5) + 1 = 11; 375 + 11 = 386$
EXTRICATE

Round 190

BLISTERED 9, BRISTLED 8, TREBLES 7
ADAPTIVE 8, AVIATED 7, DATIVE 6
IMMATURE 8, MEATIER 7, ATRIUM 6
STABILES 8, ELASTIC 7, BEASTS 6
$10 + 10 + 7 = 27; 27 \times 9 = 243; 243 + 1 = 244$
$(100 + 50) \times 7 = 1050; 75 + 25 + 8 = 108; 1050 - 108 = 942$
VALIDATED

Round 191

SAVELOYS 8, SOLVATE 7, VASTLY 6
CANDLELIT 9, CEDILLA 7, CALLED 6
SLOPPIER 8, RIPPLES 7, SAILOR 6
RECEPTION 9, ERECTION 8, PIONEER 7
$3 \times 5 \times 7 = 105; 105 + 4 + 2 = 111; 111 \times 9 = 999$
$100 - 25 + 7 = 82; 82 \times 7 = 574; 574 + 4 = 578$
DOMINATED

Round 192

LANDLORD 8, ADORNED 7, LADDER 6
BONEMEAL 8, BOATMEN 7, LAMENT 6
ACOUSTIC 8, CAUSTIC 7, CACTUS 6
PRICKLIER 9, PRICKIER 8, PICKLER 7
$100 + 75 + 2 = 177; 177 \times 4 = 708; 708 - 25 = 683$
$100 - 10 = 90; (50/10) + 1 + 1 = 7; 90 \times 7 = 630$
HORRIFIED

Round 193

PURIFIED 8, PUFFIER 7, DIFFER 6
REARWARD 8, AWARDER 7, RETARD 6
TRAGEDIAN 9, DRAINAGE 8, READING 7
CREOSOTES 9, SCOOTERS 8, STEREOS 7
$50 + 4 = 54; 10 + 7 + 1 = 18; 54 \times 18 = 972$
$(4 \times 25) - 5 = 95; 9 \times 95 = 855; 855 - (6 + 1) = 848$
PANDERING

Round 194

TANDOORI 8, OVATION 7, ORDAIN 6
REALISTIC 9, RECITALS 8, ECLAIRS 7
DESECRATE 9, DECREASE 8, CREATED 7
CAMPFIRE 8, PRIMATE 7, ARMPIT 6
$75 + 50 + 2 = 127; 127 \times 3 = 381; 381 + 25 + 1 = 407$
$(9 + 7) \times 50 = 800; 25 + 5 - 2 = 28; 800 + 28 = 828$
SUSPECTED

Round 195

HOUSEMAID 9, MADHOUSE 8, HIDEOUS 7
BOOKSHELF 9, BEFOOLS 7, BLOKES 6

447

ACCLIMATE 9, ACCLAIM 7, MALICE 6
TALISMAN 8, STAMINA 7, AWAITS 6
$(75/5) \times 6 = 90; 90 \times 6 = 540; 540 + 1 + 1 = 542$
$(3 + 4) \times (3 + 2) = 35; 35 \times 25 = 875; 875 + 7 = 882$
PROPOSING

Round 196

NAVIGABLE 9, GAINABLE 8, LEAVING 7
MEDICAL 7, MALICE 6, EDICT 5
LABOURED 8, BURGLED 7, ORDEAL 6
DRIVEWAY 8, WAVIER 6, JAWED 5
$4 \times 5 \times 4 = 80; (80 + 2) \times 8 = 656; 656 + 1 = 657$
$(75 + 25) - (6 + 2) = 92; 92 \times 9 = 828; 828 + 2 = 830$
GERIATRIC

Round 197

RATEPAYER 9, TAPERER 7, RETYPE 6
SAINTDOM 8, MASTOID 7, VOMITS 6
UNDERSEA 8, WARDENS 7, WANDER 6
FALSEHOOD 9, SELFHOOD 8, SEAFOOD 7
$(8 + 6) \times 50 = 700; (7 \times 5) - 6 = 29; 700 + 29 = 729$
$(50 + 7) \times 10 = 570; 570 - (8 - 2) = 564$
MENTALITY

Round 198

TAILGATE 8, AGITATE 7, LIGATE 6
BREAKDOWN 9, BEADWORK 8, BROWNED 7
ABSINTHE 8, LESBIAN 7, LISTEN 6
ANGRIEST 8, STINGER 7, TAXING 6
$100 + 50 - 6 = 144; 144 \times 3 = 432; 432 - (75/25) = 429$
$(8 + 1) \times 75 = 675; 5 \times (2 + 2) = 20; 675 + 20 = 695$
BLACKENED

Round 199

SAILBOAT 8, SOLATIA 7, AFLOAT 6
RAINCOAT 8, OCARINA 7, RATION 6
CALIBRATE 9, BACTERIA 8, ARTICLE 7
LAKESIDE 8, LEASHED 7, LADIES 6
$(100 + 25) - (9 - 4) = 120; 120 \times 8 = 960; 960 - 4 = 956$
$(6 \times 6) - (10 + 1) = 25; 25 \times 25 = 625; 625 + 3 = 628$
INSTIGATE

Round 200

CRINOLINE 9, INCLINER 8, ONEIRIC 7
REGIONAL 8, HALOGEN 7, LONGER 6
WHITEBAIT 9, TIBIAE 6, HABIT 5
WAISTLINE 9, LITANIES 8, SALIENT 7
$8 + (3 \times 2) = 14; (6 \times 7) \times 14 = 588; 588 + 3 = 591$
$(10 \times 25) - 8 = 242; 242 \times 3 = 726; 726 + (10/2) = 731$
PETROLEUM